100 THINGS NASCAR FANS
SHOULD KNOW & DO
BEFORE THEY DIE

Mike Hembree

TRIUMPH
BOOKS

Copyright © 2012 by Mike Hembree

No part of this publication may be reproduced, stored in a retrieval system, or transmitted in any form by any means, electronic, mechanical, photocopying, or otherwise, without the prior written permission of the publisher, Triumph Books LLC, 542 South Dearborn Street, Suite 750, Chicago, Illinois 60605.

Library of Congress Cataloging-in-Publication Data

Hembree, Michael, 1951–
  100 things NASCAR fans should know & do before they die / Mike Hembree.
     p. cm.
  Includes bibliographical references.
  ISBN 978-1-60078-670-9 (pbk.)
  1. Stock car racing—United States—History. 2. Stock car racing—United States—Miscellanea. 3. NASCAR (Association)—History.
4. NASCAR (Association)—Miscellanea. I. Title.
  GV1029.9.S74H42 2012
  796.72—dc23
                                        2011049003

This book is available in quantity at special discounts for your group or organization. For further information, contact:
  Triumph Books LLC
  542 South Dearborn Street
  Suite 750
  Chicago, Illinois 60605
  (312) 939-3330
  Fax (312) 663-3557
  www.triumphbooks.com

Printed in U.S.A.
ISBN: 978-1-60078-670-9
Design by Patricia Frey
All photos courtesy of AP Images unless otherwised noted

For Everett "Cotton" Owens, racer and friend

Contents

Foreword

The book you are holding was written by a genuine NASCAR insider—not by someone who has suddenly found NASCAR and has defined himself as an expert after having watched the sport on TV for a couple of years, but someone who knows what goes on in America's most popular racing series.

Mike Hembree has been around—in person—for a long time, and he knows what's going on in big league NASCAR, what has gone on, and he's got a good feel for what *will* go on in the future.

So as you read his *100 Things NASCAR Fans Should Know & Do Before They Die*, you can feel safe that you are getting the right stuff, the honest real deal that's as tasty as a Martinsville Speedway hot dog and as dramatic as a "big one" crash at Talladega.

Today's NASCAR continues to draw the largest crowds of any sporting event in this country. Most Sprint Cup races draw more than 100,000 souls, many of them wearing the colors of their favorite driver on the T-shirts on their backs or the caps on their heads. NASCAR TV ratings are often the top sports draw of the weekend. And new sponsors keep coming to see if the promise of fan loyalty to the brands that participate in the sport is real. It is.

Against that backdrop, today's NASCAR Sprint Cup Series is a huge draw worldwide. Nice that F-1 winner Juan Pablo Montoya came to NASCAR, nice that Indy Car's most popular driver, Danica Patrick, is moving to NASCAR, and nice that F-1 champion Kimi Raikkonen has shown enough interest to actually pay to drive for Kyle Busch Motorsports.

As you consider these 100 things to know or experience in NASCAR, be sure to note the youngsters who are coming to the sport, headlined by Trevor Bayne, who won the Daytona 500 in 2011 the day after his 20th birthday. This book will give you a start on 100 things, but NASCAR continues to grow and change, so it's only a foundation for what's likely to come next.

The sport has changed a lot in the past 10 years with the advent of the new point system, a new way the champion is decided in the top division with a Chase format, a common car that puts the races more in the hands of the drivers and their crews in two of the top three series, and new race procedures that give more drivers and teams a better chance to win the race as its end nears.

If you're just discovering NASCAR or if you have been a lifelong fan, a look at the 100 things to know or do and see is a worthwhile ride.

Dick Berggren
Executive Editor, *Speedway Illustrated* magazine
Pit reporter NASCAR on FOX

Introduction

To complete the writing of a book about stock car racing from the porch of cabin No. 6 at Lamar Buffalo Ranch in Yellowstone National Park in Wyoming is a strange feeling, indeed. That's exactly the setup, however, as I write the final numbers in this attempt to catalog the 100 things every NASCAR fan should know or do before his or her final checkered flag.

The quiet here on Yellowstone's northern range is something magical, a direct opposite of the vibrant noise of the Sprint Cup tour that I have traveled for 30 years, starting in 1975 with a break of a few years during which other pursuits of less horsepower were followed.

The only noise at the moment is produced by a strong wind—promising an afternoon storm—whipping up the Lamar Valley, which has been described as home to one of the world's richest collections of wildlife.

That also qualifies as a descriptor for the circus-like NASCAR circuit, known to attract fans whose enthusiasm for their racing is paralleled by few other collections of sports zealots. Over the course of a career following these nomads from Martinsville to Daytona and Talladega to Sonoma, I have found them to be so wildly devoted to and passionate for their sport that they will wear apparel of questionable taste in support of their favorite driver, sit in pouring rain anticipating the start of a race that will later be washed out, pay outrageously inflated hotel prices on a race weekend, and engage in heated debate—occasionally fueled by adult beverages—about the value of a particular driver, team, or track.

NASCAR is unlike most other sports in many ways.

Unlike football, baseball, basketball, hockey, and tennis, sports in which the landscape upon which the game is played is largely the same from venue to venue, NASCAR races happen on a rich variety of speedways—long, short, high-banked, flat, wide, narrow, relatively new, a century old.

The traveling carnival—complete with barkers, death-defying entertainers, and a smorgasbord of food that is both highly edible and highly caloric—that is NASCAR rolls into town for the weekend, works through practice, qualifying, and racing, and leaves to move on to another track where the challenge will be very different.

Talladega is not the same as Atlanta. Daytona is not the same as Darlington. Watkins Glen is not the same as Charlotte. Every week presents a different trial.

NASCAR also demands teamwork from an odd assortment of characters—driver, crew chief, engine builder, engineer, tire changers, jackman, spotter, aerodynamic specialist, and sponsor.

When everyone is on the same page, magic happens.

Although relatively young when viewed against most other sports, stock car racing has a rich and colorful history. It is one part Detroit, one part Southern, one part mechanical, one part bravery, and all parts adventure.

Within these pages we take a look at the highlights of that history, at the races and places that have mattered most, and at the things every fan should find important.

There's the green flag.

Mike Hembree
Yellowstone National Park, Wyoming
August 21, 2011

1 Richard Petty

Everything NASCAR starts with one name—Richard Petty.

He is the once, current, and future king of stock car racing, a man who established records that, no matter the talent of those who followed him and those yet to come, will never be broken.

More importantly, however, Petty, he of the piano-key smile, the cowboy hat, and the ever-present sunglasses, established a template for the ideal race car driver. Attending his father Lee's races as a kid, Petty quickly realized the importance of the race fan. And as he began his driving career, he made every effort to interact positively with as many fans as possible.

On many hot tough Saturday nights when he might have finished 10th in a field of 30 at some long-forgotten dirt track in the middle of Nowheresville, USA, Petty would sit and sign autographs until every interested fan had been accommodated. They all went home happy. And they were likely to return.

"It was amazing what he did," said Dale Inman, Petty's crew chief and cousin. "He did that so many times at so many places. There was always another fan waiting."

It is no overstatement to claim that the success of NASCAR in its early-growth years—from the start of the 1960s into the early 1970s—was built on Petty's strong back. There were other expert drivers, to be sure, but none carried the sizzle and pop of Petty and his winning smile. He became a cult hero.

By the late 1960s Petty had built a huge fan base, and his blue and red No. 43 race cars were among the most recognizable sights in the sports world—even among people who weren't racing fans. When Petty would travel and visit small towns, even without his

Richard Petty had a lot to smile about on February 18, 1974. He had just won the Daytona 500 for the fifth time. (AP Photo)

racing garb, word would quickly spread that he was on Main Street, and crowds would gather.

At many NASCAR circuit stops, particularly in the 1960s when the schedule was much more crowded and teams hop-scotched from one dirt track to another within a single week, the Petty Enterprises race car was a prohibitive favorite. The cars were immaculately prepared by Inman, the engines were expertly built by Maurice Petty (Richard's brother), and most in the field knew—barring mechanical collapse—that Petty would be the man to beat at race's end.

In a driving career that ran from 1958 to 1992, Petty basically wrote, designed, and numbered the NASCAR record book. He won 200 times, a Sprint Cup record that won't be touched in part because today's schedule—while still imposing with 36 races a year—can't compare with early NASCAR schedules that often had teams racing several times a week. Petty had many more chances to win—and he took a bunch of them. Inman has joked that if he had been a better crew chief, Petty would have won 400 times.

Second on the victory list is David Pearson with 105.

Despite the shine of Petty's career victory total, it is perhaps overshadowed by another of his records—10 consecutive wins during the 1967 season, a mark that is about as likely to be duplicated in today's racing as a Ford is likely to be advertised by Chevrolet.

Petty's solid blue Plymouth was a ghost not to be caught during that remarkable year, one in which he posted 27 total wins. To think of one driver winning 10 straight races in today's NASCAR environment is to be labeled goofy. Petty's streak stretched from mid-August to early October that year, and it continues to get notice from drivers attempting to follow in his tire tracks today.

"The 10 in a row, that's tough," driver Ryan Newman said. "And he did it when it was pretty tough racing back in the day."

A Family Affair

The Petty family of Level Cross, North Carolina, had a farm, and Lee Petty, the family patriarch, operated a small trucking company. But make no mistake—their business was racing.

Lee Petty, born into poverty in rural North Carolina in 1914, jumped into stock car racing at what now seems a ridiculously advanced age—35—and turned what might have appeared to be a lark into one of the most successful motorsports operations in the country.

He entered the first NASCAR Strictly Stock (now Sprint Cup) race in 1949 and created one of the fledgling sanctioning body's first spectacles by rolling his entry—a huge Buick Roadmaster—and mangling the car. It sparked the first caution period in the sport's history.

That was one of the few things the founder of Petty Enterprises did wrong in his racing and business career.

Petty started his team in an old reaper shed on his home/farm property and drove on to win 54 races (including the inaugural Daytona 500 in 1959) and three national championships. He soon involved his sons, Richard (driving) and Maurice (building engines), in the operation. Richard elevated the family business to a new level.

Eventually, Lee faded into the background and began concentrating on his golf game. Richard and Maurice took over the operation as Richard began stacking up victories and championships.

Two more generations followed. Richard's son, Kyle, joined the ranks of winning Pettys, and Kyle's son, Adam, became the fourth generation of family drivers. Sadly, Adam's promise was never realized. He was killed in a crash during practice at New Hampshire Motor Speedway in 2000, rocking NASCAR's first family to its core.

Among Petty's other NASCAR records are seven Daytona 500 victories, seven Sprint Cup championships (a record he shares with Dale Earnhardt Sr.), 1,185 starts, and 123 poles.

Twenty years after the end of his driving career, Petty, a first-round pick for the NASCAR Hall of Fame, remains the sport's grandest ambassador. He still appears at virtually every race, posing for photographs with fans, signing autographs, and simply being the King.

It's good to be the King.

Although he owns vacation homes and has any number of other interests—business and otherwise—calling for his time, Petty still wants to be at the track and be involved in garage-area goings-on. And the sport is the better for it.

2 1979 Daytona 500

The 1979 Daytona 500 has been labeled the "Race That Made NASCAR."

Its finish is remembered as one of the greatest in the sport's history—some say *the* greatest—the aftermath of that finish has been replayed thousands of times, especially when NASCAR feels the need for a publicity boost.

It started innocently enough.

Superspeedway ace Buddy Baker, who had won one of the 500's qualifiers, was considered the race favorite that February, but his engine gave up after only 38 laps. That opened the door for a number of contenders, including Donnie Allison, Darrell Waltrip, Richard Petty, Cale Yarborough, Benny Parsons, and Dale Earnhardt Sr., who was making his first start in the 500.

As the afternoon drama unfolded, the race was being beamed to a national television audience for the first time. CBS had decided to cover the race from start to finish, abandoning the practice of showing the closing portions of races, as had been the accepted approach in previous years. The networks generally feared they

A Signal from the Restroom

Although the CBS broadcast of the 1979 Daytona 500 was the first telecast of a major NASCAR race from start to finish on national television, it was not the first NASCAR major-series event to be covered live from green flag to checkered.

That distinction belongs to the Greenville 200, a 100-mile race run at historic Greenville-Pickens Speedway in northwestern South Carolina on April 10, 1971.

ABC broadcast the race from beginning to end as part of its popular Wide World of Sports anthology program. This wasn't a case of ABC showing up with its cameras on a Saturday afternoon and sending the race across the country. Weeks of preparation—and no little amount of standards-twisting—went into the broadcast. No stones were left unturned.

"About a month before the race, a guy from ABC in New York called," said Pete Blackwell, the track's longtime operator. "They had talked to Bill France, and they were looking for a race they could get in on *Wide World of Sports* in an hour and a half. They had gone through results sheets and saw that we had finished a race in about an hour and 25 minutes. So the guy asked me if I thought we could do that again. I said, 'Sure,' although there was no way I could be sure."

Greenville-Pickens, originally a horse-racing facility (like some other stock car racing tracks), was one of NASCAR's bedrock speedways. Blackwell was a reliable promoter and track manager who could be counted on to host a good race.

The agreement was reached, and NASCAR officials, cooperating with ABC's desire to have the race fit into the 90-minute window for *Wide World of Sports*, cut the starting field from 30 cars to 26, thus theoretically reducing the possibility of caution flags and speeding up the race progress.

Workers erected scaffolding around the perimeter of the track for cameras, and a portable studio was set up near the first turn for announcers Jim McKay, who would become one of ABC's most famous sports journalists, and Chris Economaki, whose name would become synonymous with major motorsports events. Economaki made many other appearances on televised motorsports programs over the years and also became one of racing's greatest print journalists.

Perhaps the most important person on site that day, however, was a technician who was in charge of directing the feed from the track to ABC headquarters in New York City. Because of limited space at the track, he was stationed in one of the track's restrooms.

Bobby Isaac won the race in one hour and 16 minutes (there was only one caution flag), giving broadcasters extra time to fill at the end of the event. Fears of the race running long were unrealized.

The day was judged a success, and NASCAR's live television era had begun.

could not sustain interest in a race that could stretch significantly longer than three hours.

CBS executives could not have known that they had chosen the perfect 500 to cover from green flag to checkered. A heavy snowstorm blanketed much of the East Coast that weekend, giving broadcasters a captive audience for the race. Many viewers who had a casual interest at best in NASCAR tuned in because they had little else to do—and could go nowhere—on a miserable winter afternoon.

As the closing miles approached, it was clear that barring a mechanical failure or an accident, the race probably would be decided between Donnie Allison and Cale Yarborough, two of the sport's best drivers. Petty, Waltrip, and A.J. Foyt also had strong cars, but they were about a half-lap behind Allison and Yarborough with several laps remaining.

Yarborough was running second to Allison entering the final lap, and he made his move to pass on the backstretch. Yarborough, whose car appeared to be slightly better than Allison's, charged to the inside, but Allison moved down to block. Yarborough, who knew that backing off to avoid the block would probably cost him the race, stayed on the throttle. The two cars hit, then Yarborough turned up into Allison again, sending both cars into the outside wall. As they lost speed, they spiraled down the track banking and onto the infield apron. The two favorites suddenly were sidelined.

Fans in the grandstands and in living rooms across the country quickly realized that someone else was going to win the race. And the man who inherited the lead was one of Daytona's best, although he hadn't won a NASCAR event anywhere in the past 45 races.

His name was Richard Petty.

As Yarborough and Allison sat in their battered vehicles and tried to come to grips with what had happened, Petty sprinted to the lead. Waltrip closed on his bumper as they entered the fourth turn for the final time, but he had no shot to pass. Petty took his sixth Daytona 500 checkered flag with Waltrip in his wake.

Meanwhile, back in the third-turn area, tempers were flaring. Bobby Allison, Donnie's brother and also a competitor in the race, had stopped at the crash site to check on him. Yarborough and Donnie were having a not-very-pleasant conversation about the accident, and Yarborough walked over to Bobby's car. They exchanged words, and Yarborough hit Bobby with his helmet. Bobby climbed out of his car, and he and Yarborough engaged in a brief scuffle before track workers separated them.

Network cameras carried a few moments of the tussle.

The fight was water-cooler fodder across the country for much of the following week, and NASCAR picked up the sort of publicity that millions of dollars couldn't buy.

Yarborough would go on to win the Daytona 500 in 1983 and 1984 before retiring in 1988. Donnie Allison never won the 500 and still lists that winter day as one of his biggest regrets in racing. Richard Petty won the race for the seventh and final time in 1981.

One of the most popular exhibits in the NASCAR Hall of Fame in Charlotte, North Carolina, recreates that day and one of the most dynamic finishes in the sport's history.

3 Founding: Smoke-Filled Room, Part One

It was the Christmas season in 1947, but several dozen men who had gathered near the Atlantic shore in Daytona Beach, Florida, weren't there for holiday activities.

All had been summoned to a series of meetings by racer and dreamer Bill France Sr. France, who had been involved in auto racing in one form or another since the 1930s (with the exception of the World War II years), was bringing together most of the people he considered important in the stock car motorsports world to talk some turkey.

France's somewhat grandiose concept of the gathering was to determine what he called "the outcome of stock car racing in the country today."

France, who dreamed no small dreams, saw the wild meanderings of the stock car racing world and wanted to bring all the loose ends together in a single ruling organization—one that he would control.

There were various small groups running ragtag racing series here and there. France was among the promoters trying to put down roots with a form of racing that would be accepted across the board as respectable and organized. He found out how hard that process was in 1946 when, while trying to promote one of his races in Charlotte, North Carolina, as a "national championship" event, he was told by local newspaper sports editor Wilton Garrison that he had to have a legitimate national-level organization with standards, rules, and point standings before mainstream media outlets would accept his winning drivers as "national champions."

Later that year, France formed the National Championship Stock Car Circuit, and he promoted races under its banner in 1946 and 1947.

With that first step taken, France called the December 1947 meetings in Daytona Beach to exchange ideas with other promoters, drivers, and mechanics and hopefully start an umbrella organization that would control much of stock car racing in the nation.

Perhaps not surprisingly, considering those in attendance, the meetings were held in a bar—the Ebony Room atop the Streamline Hotel located on Daytona's beachside highway. There was plenty to drink, and France arranged for a few local women to hang around and entertain those in attendance.

There was response from across the stock car racing landscape. Among those who answered France's summons were promoters Joe Littlejohn and Bill Tuthill, drivers Marshall Teague, Ed Samples, Buddy Shuman, and Red Byron, and ace mechanic Red Vogt.

Participants in the meeting were interviewed sporadically in the years that followed. They often disagreed about the number of men who attended, but it is likely that at least 22 and possibly as many as 35 attended one or more of the sessions over a four-day period. It's quite likely that several uninvited guests popped in and out of the sessions because the Streamline was a popular stopping point for those involved in racing on the beach.

Tuthill, a France confidant, ran the meetings, but France clearly was the central figure.

Among the drivers present was Sam Packard, who had moved south from Rhode Island to race on the Daytona beach-road course. He said the meeting included "Yankees, Southerners, and bootleggers. We all more or less knew each other. We had been running tracks together. We were all after the same thing."

Benny Kahn, longtime sports journalist in Daytona Beach, also attended the meetings. He described participants as "the owner of a small local filling station; a local race driver; a Providence, Rhode Island, motorcycle dealer; an Atlanta garage operator; a Spartanburg turnip farmer; a New Rochelle, New York, midget racetrack

Well, Maybe Just One Drink

The organizational meetings that resulted in the formation of NASCAR lasted over portions of four days in December 1947. The meetings called by promoter Bill France Sr. were held in the Ebony Lounge, a bar atop the Streamline Hotel in Daytona Beach, Florida.

Why did the meetings stretch across four days? Couldn't the hows and whys and details have been handled in one long meeting? Sam Packard, a driver who was in attendance, had a quick explanation for the extended conversations.

"Well, this was in a cocktail lounge," he said.

promoter; a moonshiner or two with anonymous addresses; and assorted hustlers."

Kahn probably was right on the money (although everyone in attendance probably was a hustler of one sort or another).

While France's primary goal was to establish an over-arcing organization to run stock car racing, many of the other participants probably were most concerned about bringing some monetary control to the sport. Many drivers had the experience of winning a race only to visit the track's payoff window and find the promoter missing, having raced out of town with the gate receipts.

"We thought the whole thing should have some teeth in it," said Joe Littlejohn, who had raced on the beach and promoted races in the Carolinas. "People were racing, and they had to have some rules and regulations and someone to enforce them."

Photographs of the initial meeting show the participants gathered around a row of tables, with cigarette smoke hanging in the air.

To no one's surprise, France was elected the organization's president. Then talk turned to a name for the group. Those voting initially picked National Stock Car Racing Association, but Vogt told the group that a sanctioning organization in Georgia was already using that name. By late afternoon, a second vote had been taken, and Vogt's suggestion—National Association of Stock Car Auto Racing—was chosen. The "of" later was changed to "for."

Two months later, with the help of another France friend, Daytona Beach lawyer Louis Ossinsky, the organization was incorporated. France, Tuthill, and Ossinsky were the original stockholders. Promoter Ed Otto later owned some shares, but France eventually bought full ownership.

The spadework had been done, and France launched into the detail work. He hired office staff. NASCAR's first office was located in the France home at 29 Goodall Avenue in Daytona Beach. Later, it moved to a facility on Main Street. Today it has offices in several locations across the country, although headquarters remains in Daytona Beach.

NASCAR membership initially cost $10, a price that bought the member a membership card, a car decal, a pin, a newsletter, and $10 worth of coupons, each good for 50 cents off race admission.

France had started the engines.

4 Winston: Smoke-Filled Room, Part Two

The tides of change were swirling around NASCAR as the 1960s turned into the 1970s.

And there was none bigger than the arrival on the stock car racing scene of the R.J. Reynolds Tobacco Co. and its Winston cigarette brand. How those smokes became such a big part of NASCAR, reaching into virtually every corner of its business, is an unusual story.

It began with team owner Junior Johnson. After the federal government banned tobacco advertising from television, Johnson, who lived within easy driving distance of the company's head-quarters in Winston-Salem, North Carolina, figured RJR officials would have some extra money to spend on other publicity vehicles, so he thought they might be interested in planting cigarette advertising on his race cars.

Johnson met with RJR representatives and made his pitch. He discovered that RJR had a boatload of money to spend, much more than it could spend on a single team. He suggested the executives meet with NASCAR, and Bill France Sr. and Bill France Jr. soon arrived for talks.

In December 1970 Reynolds was announced as the primary sponsor of NASCAR's lead series (then known as Grand National). The name was changed to Winston Cup Grand National (and later to simply Winston Cup), and a journey of more than three decades began.

The arrival of Winston revolutionized NASCAR. Sports marketing executives with the company suggested that NASCAR trim its race schedule to a more manageable total for 1972, thus enabling the sanctioning body and its new sponsor to better publicize and support bigger races. The schedule dropped from 48 races to 31. Almost immediately more attention and much more money were given to the seasonal champion.

The first evidence of Winston's arrival on the NASCAR scene was the bright red of the showy uniforms Winston's representatives wore at the track. Unleashed on the sport to assist at all levels of public relations, the Winston gang became as familiar at NASCAR events as fried chicken and beer.

RJR boosted the sport in countless other ways, including enlarging purses significantly, sponsoring ancillary events, providing paint and other incidentals to spruce up speedways, and bringing fans closer to racing with contests and public appearances by drivers and others. NASCAR became fertile ground for the promotional ideas of men like Ralph Seagraves and T. Wayne

Robertson, RJR executives who became key advisors to the France family and important figures as racing grew.

Winston's arrival was also important because of the doors it opened for other sponsors. For much of its history, NASCAR had received the majority of its sponsorship and advertising support from automotive-related companies. Winston's early success attracted other non-automotive sponsors.

Reynolds' run with NASCAR ended in 2004 as Nextel—later Sprint—became the series' primary sponsor.

5 Dale Earnhardt Sr.

Dale Earnhardt Sr. grew up watching his father, noted short-track driver Ralph Earnhardt, work on race cars deep into the night in the garage behind the modest Earnhardt home in the textile village of Kannapolis, North Carolina.

This fascinated Dale. After nights when his father was away at some short track dusting the competition, Dale would walk to the garage early the next morning and generally could tell how Ralph had done based on the amount of dirt and mud on the car and how many dings its sheet metal had absorbed.

Helping his dad in the shop, Dale didn't need a lot of debate to decide that he liked working on race cars much more than school. In the ninth grade, he dropped out.

That was a life's course that he recommended against every time he had the chance to speak to kids later in life, but for Earnhardt it began the long road to riches and fame. It was a detour to greatness.

He helped his father in the shop, learned the basics of preparing cars for competition, and began contemplating a driving career of his own. Connecting the dots between the dream and the reality, though, was difficult. Earnhardt had much more desire than money. In the end, that made the Earnhardt story all the more remarkable, however, and helped solidify him as a working man's hero, a champion to millions who saw themselves in him.

Earnhardt graduated from the hard-knocks school of small-town North Carolina and became one of the world's most famous race car drivers, acquiring riches, and reputation along the way and becoming one of NASCAR's most marketable competitors.

He also put up big numbers: 76 Sprint Cup victories, seven national championships, 34 wins at Daytona International Speedway, $42 million in career winnings, and untold millions in sponsor and endorsement dollars. He was an easy choice among the first five individuals elected to the NASCAR Hall of Fame.

Through an aggressive—much too aggressive, some said—driving style and a menacing presence, Earnhardt built a huge fan base that became as devoted as any in sports. Fans bought his caps and T-shirts by the truckloads, and they proudly held up three fingers—his number—at the track. They named their children Dale and tattooed his car and his profile on their arms (and other body parts). They made pilgrimages to his "Garage Mahal" shop in Mooresville, North Carolina, both before and after his death.

He was a folk hero, the Elvis of his sport. His last lap came on the final lap of the 2001 Daytona 500, and the sport grieved. It had lost its competitive heart.

"Dale was really a self-made guy," NASCAR historian Buz McKim said. "He started out with nothing. Ralph had nothing to pass on to him. Dale made it on his own with little education but a lot of determination and talent.

"He'll be the guy looked on forever as the working man's man."

Few things better illustrate Earnhardt's struggle to make it in NASCAR than his debut. That came on May 25, 1975, in one of

Dale Earnhardt receives a trophy after winning the Busch 420 on July 17, 1983, at Nashville International Raceway. (AP Photo)

NASCAR's toughest races, the World 600 (now the Coca-Cola 600) at Charlotte Motor Speedway.

Earnhardt had made a reputation for himself by bumping around Carolina's short tracks and doing well with marginal equipment. He was targeting the big time, but he had no money to pursue it.

Through the intervention of a friend, Norman Negre, he got a ride in the 600. Ed Negre, Norman's father, owned a Cup team and was a regular driver in the series. Norman talked his father into letting Earnhardt drive a second team Dodge in the 600, a decision Ed Negre made only after telling his son he and Earnhardt had to prepare the car.

They jumped at the chance.

It was a comedy of sorts. Earnhardt had never raced in an event even close to the length of the CMS marathon, and he made one pit stop simply to pick up a drink of water, an incident that his competitors would find very amusing when it was recounted later in his career. He finished 22nd, 45 laps down, and no one paid much notice.

Four years later, his reputation as an up-and-coming driver established by strong runs in the Busch Series, Earnhardt ran for Cup rookie of the year and won the award. The next season, to the surprise of many, he won the Cup championship.

During that rookie season, he won for the first time, visiting victory lane at Bristol Motor Speedway in April in just his 16th start.

"This is a bigger thrill than my first-ever racing victory," Earnhardt said that day. "This was a win in the big leagues against the top-caliber drivers. It wasn't some dirt track back at home."

Earnhardt won five times the next season, scoring his first superspeedway victory at Atlanta, and was consistent enough throughout the year to notch his first championship—for team owner Rod Osterlund.

Earnhardt was shocked the next year when Osterlund suddenly decided to leave the sport, selling his team to businessman J.D. Stacy. The move defined the rest of Earnhardt's career—and in a positive way. That summer Earnhardt quit Stacy, whose ties to racing were tenuous, and joined a team owned by journeyman driver Richard Childress, who was ready to turn over the driver's seat in his cars to someone else.

Earnhardt and Childress became fast friends, and they would become faster racers. But Childress did not yet have the resources needed to match Earnhardt's skills, and after that partial season, Earnhardt moved on to drive two years for Spartanburg, South Carolina, team owner Bud Moore.

"He was the world's greatest," said Moore, like Earnhardt a member of the NASCAR Hall of Fame. "He was the type of driver, like Junior Johnson, who was there to win the race.

"When he first started driving for me, I told him, 'Now, Dale, what you need to do is think about this track, this car, and what's going on. Don't be thinking about some gal or something else. You keep your eye on that track and learn how to run it. Learn different grooves and the feel of the car. Study your competition.'

"Then I told him to pass that guy on the high side or on the low side or run over him. And that's what he did."

In 1984, Childress felt he was ready to build consistently impressive cars for Earnhardt, and they reunited. The result was one of the best partnerships ever at NASCAR's top level. Earnhardt and Childress won their first championship together in 1986, and Earnhardt won $1 million in a season for the first time.

Another championship followed in 1987 and a fourth in 1990. Earnhardt also won the Cup title in 1991, 1993, and 1994.

Earnhardt became known as the Intimidator, a nickname that sold truckloads of T-shirts. Although few of his contemporaries admitted to buying into the Intimidator persona—and none would

The Man In What?

One of several nicknames Dale Earnhardt Sr. picked up over a long and successful driving career was the Man in Black. For most of his career, he drove a black No. 3 Chevrolet fielded by Richard Childress Racing. Although the car had numerous paint schemes over the years, it was solid black through most of Earnhardt's golden years.

The Earnhardt racing story began, however, in quite another shade of the color wheel. His first race car, a 1956 Ford that carried the number K-2, was painted shocking pink.

admit to being intimidated by him, Earnhardt often validated the thinking that he would do anything to win.

He smashed Terry Labonte on the last lap to win a race at Bristol. He engaged Geoff Bodine in a classic series of "Southern boy versus Yankee" duels. He sent Rusty Wallace into a spectacular flipping crash at Talladega, a wreck that stuck in Wallace's craw for a long time. He tangled with Georgia golden boy and fellow fan favorite Bill Elliott on the high ground of the Winston All-Star Race.

"He was good, but he had a lot of people who would just pull over and let him by because he had hit so many of them," said retired driver David Pearson, who raced with and for Earnhardt. "He liked to have killed Rusty Wallace four or five times. When it came down to it, he was going to hit you or knock you out of the way and say he didn't mean to or something like that. A lot of times, he'd spin people out when he didn't have to.

"I borrowed some rims from him one time. He said, 'You better put them on pretty good because I'm going to knock them off.' He knew who he could run over."

The biggest moment of Earnhardt's career came in February 1998 when he finally defeated the demons that had bedeviled him in the Daytona 500 for 20 years. In one of the most popular and most celebrated victories ever by any NASCAR driver, Earnhardt won the 500 to end two decades of misery in NASCAR's biggest race.

"The monkey is off my back!" he yelled as he entered the Daytona International Speedway press box for the winner's interview. Earnhardt had won 30 races at Daytona entering that 500, but he had been slapped around by all manner of bad luck—including a flat tire in the third turn while leading on the last lap—in the event.

Earnhardt's last victory—in the October 2000 race at Talladega Superspeedway—was one of the most remarkable of the 76 Cup wins he scored. He sprinted through the Talladega draft over the final five laps like a missile on a mission, firing forward from 18th to win in an impressive display of drafting proficiency.

In an interview seven months before his death, Earnhardt talked about his pursuit of what would have been a record eighth Cup championship.

"I've got four years of racing left, at least," he said. "Who knows, I might even drive another car with my own team. I'm not ruling anything out. I've got a job and an opportunity to win that eighth championship. That's what we're focusing on. That's what we're driving for. That's what we're working for.

"I'm excited about what I do. I'm not content with not winning. If somebody tells you I'm riding my years out, they're not paying attention."

Earnhardt seldom talked about his NASCAR debut in Norman Negre's car, but that day became important over the years as the Earnhardt career advanced. And it became somewhat valuable for Negre. Diecast model makers produced cars based on Earnhardt's entry that day, and they were popular among Earnhardt's fan base.

Negre said later he made more money from those sales than in his driving career.

6 David Pearson

David Pearson grew up in a textile village—generally known as the "mill hill"—near Spartanburg, South Carolina, and might have followed many of his generation into the Whitney cotton factory that was the town's heart.

However, as a teenager, that wasn't Pearson's idea of a future. He had been to the local speedway, a half-mile dirt track on the grounds of the Piedmont Interstate Fair in Spartanburg, and watched the wild young men of the post–World War II generation kick up dust and bang fenders in fast jalopies.

"That," Pearson would say many years later, "is what I wanted to do."

There was no question in his mind that he could do it. Like so many other drivers in his era, Pearson was convinced of his abilities. He just needed a chance.

Against the odds, Pearson made it to the top levels of racing, and when he got there he performed better than most of his contemporaries and most of the drivers who traveled the same NASCAR roads.

In a career that stretched from 1960 to 1986, Pearson won 105 Sprint Cup races, second all-time only to Richard Petty, who won 200 and had more than twice as many starts as Pearson—1,185 for Petty vs. 574 for Pearson.

Pearson won three Cup championships—1966, '68, and '69—one for each of the years in which he competed seriously for the title. For much of his career, particularly in the 1970s and 1980s, Pearson ran only selected events, as he or his teams chose big-money, prestige races instead of racing for points and championships.

He got his start on the short tracks of the Carolinas, where his success in Sportsman-level racing earned him the nickname "David the Giant Killer."

He moved into Cup racing in 1960 and won the division's Rookie of the Year award that season. But it was the following year that presented Pearson with the opportunity to show that he was a driver apart from most of the rest. Someone gave him the chance.

The big break came from Ray Fox, one of the best mechanics of the era. He had a vacancy in his car's seat for the upcoming World 600 (now the Coca-Cola 600) at Charlotte Motor Speedway and didn't have any serious candidates.

Fox didn't know that much about Pearson, but he had heard the name, and the driver was highly recommended by fellow Spartanburg residents and NASCAR circuit regulars Bud Moore, Cotton Owens, and Joe Littlejohn. Fox called Pearson, who was roofing a house in Spartanburg, and offered him the ride for the 600.

The offer was one of many things Pearson wasn't slow about over the years. He jumped at the opportunity.

Pearson wasn't lacking in confidence when he showed up in Charlotte to drive the Fox Pontiac. He had never been in a race car at speeds at that level, but he wasn't intimidated. "I figure the car didn't know who was driving it," Pearson said. "If they could do it, I could."

And he did. He burned up the track in practice and brought the car in to talk to Fox. Fox asked him how the car felt. "I don't know," Pearson said. "I don't know how it's supposed to feel."

He figured that out quickly in the race, leading 225 of the 400 laps in NASCAR's longest event. And he kept his cool at race's end, driving the last two laps with a punctured tire but still winning easily over Fireball Roberts, who finished in second place.

Ray Fox had a driver, and Pearson had a future.

Where Are My Shoes?

One of the reasons David Pearson was so successful in NASCAR history was because he raced for decades without sustaining a serious injury. Pearson was an expert at avoiding accidents. He raced for more than a quarter-century without being taken to a hospital because of a racing crash.

That doesn't mean Pearson wasn't scared by a wreck, however.

In 1969, he was involved in a vicious crash at Bristol (Tennessee) Motor Speedway. He wasn't hurt, but when he looked down at the floorboard after the wreck, he discovered that the impact had knocked off his shoes.

"I always heard that people who were killed in wrecks had their shoes knocked off," Pearson said. "So it scared me for a minute."

He won two more big-track races—at Daytona and Atlanta—that season, confirming what observers had seen at Charlotte, and his reputation was set. Before the decade was over, Pearson won series championships with Owens in Dodges and with the highly respected Holman-Moody team in Fords.

In the 1970s he scored his biggest successes—although no championships—in one of the greatest partnerships in NASCAR history. Pearson and the Stuart, Virginia–based Wood Brothers team, one of NASCAR's bedrock operations, ran like wildfire through the circuit's superspeedways, challenging at virtually every stop and winning at many.

Pearson joined the Woods in 1972, and in 1973 they enjoyed stunning success on NASCAR's big tracks, winning in 11-of-18 appearances. Across the rest of the decade, they wrestled Richard Petty and his Petty Enterprises team for supremacy on the super-speedways. Petty and Pearson were the giants of the era, and they wound up finishing first and second in 63 races (Pearson led that category in wins, 33–30).

Pearson will be remembered as one of NASCAR's smartest drivers. He was not of the hard-charger school; instead, he saved his car during the early portions of races and had strong equipment for the concluding laps. On more than a few occasions, he "rallied" from deep in the pack during the final 50 miles to score wins.

At the peak of his career, Pearson, whose black hair turned gray prematurely, picked up the nickname the Silver Fox, in part for his appearance and in part for the intelligent and sly way he ran races.

He had come a long way from the David the Giant Killer days.

After his driving career ended, Pearson remained around racing by starting a Nationwide Series team that involved his sons Larry, Ricky, and Eddie. After that enterprise ended, Pearson built a vintage short-track racer and drove it to 14 victories.

7 Bill France Sr.: A Guiding Hand, an Iron Fist

It took an individual with the tough will and bright ideas of Bill France Sr. to make an audacious idea like NASCAR work.

When France, a sometimes driver and sometimes race promoter, began eyeing the development of a large national racing organization in the years after World War II, stock car racing was an untamed wild animal with little discipline or coordination. On more than a few occasions, winning drivers left tracks with no purse money because the race organizer had hit the road early. There was profit in the racing business, but a lot of it went to unscrupulous promoters.

France built a corral around the sport, named it NASCAR, and moved forward. And most of the rest of stock car racing followed him like the Pied Piper.

In the subsequent decades, he was *the man* in the world's No. 1 stock car racing series, and he turned back every effort to challenge his authority. He took on all comers and conquered every one.

Driver Bobby Allison, a tough guy in his own right, went up against France several times after a rule dispute of one sort or another and met the wall that France often erected.

"He probably was one of the most personally forceful persons I ever met," Allison said. "He just demanded that people support whatever the activity was he was involved in at that particular day and time. He had a way of demanding the support without making people turn away.

"He wouldn't compromise. It would be, 'No, we're going to do it my way, and you're going to help me.' He really had an unusual quality about him from that standpoint."

The most significant accomplishment of France's life probably occurred in Daytona Beach, Florida, near Christmas 1947 when he brought together several dozen stock car racing notables—drivers, mechanics, promoters—and talked them into forming NASCAR and putting him in position to run it.

After World War II, the nation was ready to be amused and entertained, and the automobile would play a big role in that. Veterans returning from the battle theaters settled down to start families, and soon many were able to buy the family's first car. They were ready to hit the road, to see the country, and to experience new things.

Stock car racing already was an attraction at various short tracks across the country, but there was very little solid organization. Schedules were willy-nilly. Tracks were often ragged and poorly maintained.

There were so many promoters attempting to run races in so many parts of the country, each claiming to name a "national" champion, that there was much more confusion than noteworthy competition. Racing needed a figure of authority to step in and wrestle the ragtag sport to the ground, give it a bath, straighten its clothes, and send it forward. It needed a big, big man.

France accepted that role. He was big—6'6" tall—and impressive enough physically to attract attention and respect.

France, who had been organizing races along the Daytona beachfront and at short tracks in numerous locations, ramrodded the formation of NASCAR in December 1947 and was its president through the 1971 season, when he handed the keys to his son, Bill France Jr.

France Sr. also was the visionary behind the construction of Daytona International Speedway and Talladega Superspeedway and the organization of International Speedway Corp., one of motorsports' leading speedway ownership groups.

He built the framework for everything that the sport would become, masterfully balancing the needs and demands of drivers, team owners, promoters, and the automobile industry to amass a personal fortune and start a family enterprise that has stretched into three generations and is one of international sports' most successful.

France, the son of a banker, was born September 26, 1909, in Washington, D.C. He played basketball at Central High School, but his real interest was in the fast race cars circling the old board race track at nearby Laurel, Maryland. As a teenager, he slipped away from home periodically to run the family car on that track, and a lifelong love affair was born.

After high school, France worked as a mechanic in several Washington area shops. In 1931, he married Anne Bledsoe, a nurse from North Carolina who had trained in Washington.

Tired of the Washington winters and interested in expanding his life beyond that of a mechanic, France moved his family south in 1934, settling in Daytona Beach. Apparently mainly by coincidence, he happened to land in a community bedazzled by speed. Men (and women) were racing fast cars on the hard-packed

One Sport, One Family

Founded in 1947 and incorporated in 1948, NASCAR has been under the control of one family—the Frances—since the beginning. Founder William Henry Getty "Bill Sr." France handed the presidency of the organization to his son William Clifton "Bill Jr." France in 1972. Bill Jr. served until 2000, when he named Mike Helton as his successor.

But that certainly did not end the France family's leadership role.

Brian Z. France, son of Bill Jr., became NASCAR chairman in October 2003. Jim France, Bill Jr.'s brother, is vice chairman and executive vice president of NASCAR. Lesa France Kennedy, daughter of Bill Jr., is vice chairwoman and executive vice president of NASCAR. Betty Jane France, Bill Jr.'s widow, also is a NASCAR executive vice president.

sand of the Atlantic beachfront, and France, who went to work as a mechanic and later opened his own Daytona Beach service station, jumped in with both feet.

By 1936, France was racing cars on the beach and at short tracks in the region. He quickly became a big gun in racing and business circles in the area and took over promotion of the beach races when the city of Daytona Beach, the previous sponsor, failed to produce profits. Among the lap leader awards France, ever the imaginative promoter, offered at a 1938 beach race were a bottle of rum, $2.50 credit at a local men's clothing store, a box of cigars, and a case of motor oil.

France was working toward refining his racing interests in 1941 when World War II started, effectively shutting down most motorsports activities. During the war, he worked for Daytona Boat Works, building submarine chasers.

When racing resumed after the war, France was in a prime position. He had experience driving race cars and promoting racing events. He knew all sides of the business. Daytona Beach, having already established itself as a major motorsports area prior to the war years, quickly became alive again with the sound of racing engines, and events there soon attracted daredevil drivers from all over the country. France was right in the middle of it—and poised to assume control.

By 1947, France had formed what he called the National Stock Car Racing Circuit and advertised his events in motorsports publications. He promoted events at tracks in Greensboro, North Carolina; North Wilkesboro, North Carolina; Birmingham, Alabama; Greenville, South Carolina; Columbia, South Carolina; and Trenton, New Jersey. There was competition from other race promoters, however, and it was to France's advantage to try to put himself in a leading—if not commanding—position.

That led him to call the December 1947 organizational meetings that resulted in NASCAR and his presidency of same. The participants responded to France's urging. "Stock car racing has got distinct possibilities for Sunday shows," he told those in the first meeting. "We do not know how big it can be if it's handled properly. I believe stock car racing can become a nationally recognized sport having a national points standing which will embrace the majority of large stock car events."

NASCAR was incorporated on February 21, 1948, but France ran the entity's first event six days before the incorporation became official. He and his wife, Anne, began building the foundation of the organization, advertising for NASCAR memberships first from their home and later from a small office on Main Street in Daytona Beach.

NASCAR sanctioned other races, but France's core idea—to race new American-built sedans in long-distance events—built the organization's reputation. That series—then called Strictly Stock, now Sprint Cup—began June 19, 1949, in Charlotte, North Carolina.

As the sport grew and changed during those first years, France seemed to be able to respond appropriately to every challenge.

"He knew exactly when and how to change things when they needed changing," said pioneer mechanic and team owner Bud

Moore, who like France was also a member of the NASCAR Hall of Fame. "It wasn't only with the meetings with the car owners and drivers to help take NASCAR along. He had a lot of meetings with the promoters.

"There are only a few of us who were around when he started the sport who are still here. Not that many people remember all of it. But he catered to all the teams real well. He'd come to you and ask about different things, things he could do to help the sport."

The France process became known as a benevolent dictatorship. He ruled things with a strong arm but knew that he needed successful team owners, drivers, and track promoters to make things work.

"He was pretty charismatic, and he could schmooze you pretty good," NASCAR historian Buz McKim said. "He knew he had to take care of the guys putting the show on. He would slide them a little money under the table to get them home from a race.

"Being a former driver, he knew what the guys went through. In his own way, he was kind of sympathetic toward them. He had a way of getting a lot of loyalty out of people around him."

Ultimately, France would have to deal with driver boycotts, union organizers, car manufacturer boycotts, speedway financial problems, and a long list of other difficulties, but the sport continued to grow and evolve. France was there to deal with every problem, and he normally had a proper solution.

"He was incredibly protective of his baby," McKim said.

Current NASCAR president Mike Helton said France's intimidating style "certainly helped, and I don't think he abused that, but I certainly think that was an advantage he had of getting others to see what he saw. In doing all of that, it heightened his impact. I think he had that characteristic that drew people in. He was able to share the concepts and visions and motivate them to believe in it and to work on it. When he was there holding court, so to speak, you knew that there was an authority."

France retired as NASCAR president in 1972 but remained around the sport in a variety of capacities for several more years. He died June 7, 1992, after suffering from Alzheimer's disease.

8 Cale Yarborough

Cale Yarborough, who grew up rough-and-tumble in the South Carolina backwoods, is almost always in the discussion when topics like Best Driver Ever come up. Yarborough won 83 Cup races and three Cup championships. He was the first driver to win three straight titles (1976–78).

Even gaudy numbers don't tell the full story of Yarborough's run through stock car racing, however. He was an especially tough and resilient driver, one who drove hard every lap but still had the verve and energy at the end of the race to challenge for the win.

Other drivers might have been faster or better strategists or more in tune with their equipment, but Yarborough had a distinct knack for running well and knowing where to be and what to do over the final five laps of a race. Although he lost a few last-lap battles over the course of a stellar career that stretched from 1957 to 1988, it was never smart to bet against Yarborough in a final-lap scenario.

He was gritty, and he welcomed the challenges associated with earning success in a 500-mile race on a hot summer day at a tough track. He drove hard—harder than most. Yarborough was not a "save the race car" guy.

"I've seen Cale drive cars that I didn't think anybody could drive," said retired team owner Junior Johnson, whose cars Yarborough drove when he won the consecutive championships.

Cale Yarborough brought a dirty face and a winning car into the winner's circle at Dover Downs on Sunday, May 20, 1974, after race leader Richard Petty lost an engine with only four laps remaining. Yarborough and Petty were the leaders throughout the race. (AP Photo)

"And he would not quit. I think if he was in a situation where he had to get out of a race car because of his stamina, it would be the most embarrassing thing that ever happened to him.

"He was the most determined. There was no end to his will-power. He stood apart. He was smart. He was kind of 'sneaky' brave. He just had a lot going for him."

That was not the case when Yarborough started on the racing road, however.

He grew up in rural Sardis, South Carolina, near Darlington Raceway. He was a star athlete at Timmonsville High School and was offered football scholarships, but he was attracted to the racing at Darlington so he chose fast cars as his ticket. He piled up short-track wins on small dirt tracks in South Carolina and then made his unofficial Cup debut in the 1957 Southern 500 before he was officially old enough to race.

Five years later, he was still struggling to stretch his dollars and keep racing. He and his wife, Betty Jo, were practically out of money as they traveled from their home in Sardis to Savannah, Georgia, for a short-track race. She made sandwiches to take on the trip. Yarborough had $10 in his pocket.

He lost that when he was stopped for speeding in Walterboro, South Carolina. He still thought they'd be okay, but he forgot about the toll bridge leading into Savannah. The toll was 50 cents. Betty Jo searched under the car seats and found 37 cents.

Yarborough, apparently a very convincing 22-year-old, talked the toll collector into letting them pass with the promise that he would pay the remaining 13 cents on the way back home—from the race winnings.

That strategy failed when Yarborough's car blew an engine. He didn't win any money. He borrowed $20 from the track promoter and stopped at the toll bridge on the way back to South Carolina to pay the collector.

Three years later, Yarborough won in the Cup series for the first time—at a short track in Valdosta, Georgia, after sleeping in his car to save money on a motel.

In 1968, Yarborough scored a major victory, winning the Southern 500 at his home track—Darlington—on a brutally hot Labor Day afternoon. Photographs from victory lane that day show an exhausted and grimy Yarborough finally enjoying the fruits of a career that started on a wing and a prayer. It was clear he had given everything he had that day to reach the top.

Yarborough would retire from driving two decades later and $5 million richer and with the respect of all who raced against him.

"Cale didn't know a lot about a car, and he didn't complain much about how a car handled," said Darrell Waltrip, perhaps Yarborough's biggest rival. "He just got in it and tried to make up the difference, and I've seen him do just that many times.

"I've seen him take the worst-handling car and be very competitive and win with it. He drove it as fast as he could. He was 110 percent up on the wheel all the time. He was an incredible wheelman and strong as an ox. He didn't give out. He didn't get tired."

Yarborough, who said he learned about discipline and hard work growing up on a farm, stayed in great physical condition. "If you come down with 10 laps to go and you're battling somebody who's given completely out, your odds are pretty good if you're still strong physically and mentally," Yarborough said.

Yarborough amassed three huge championship trophies and hundreds of other awards during a long career in racing. Many were destroyed in a fire at his Florence, South Carolina, automobile dealership in 1988 and in a propane tank explosion at the workshop near his home in 2007.

Yarborough did not try to replace them with duplicates. "It wouldn't be the same," he said. "None of it would have the blood, sweat, and tears in it."

He knew all about those, having seen it all as he carved out a special niche for himself in stock car racing.

9 1976 Daytona 500

The finish of the 1979 Daytona 500—with Richard Petty winning as the Allison brothers (Bobby and Donnie) wrestled with Cale Yarborough after a last-turn crash—is remembered by many fans as the ultimate climax of a NASCAR race.

But many serious historians of the sport, while acknowledging the significance of the 1979 race in spurring new national interest in NASCAR, instead look to the 1976 Daytona 500 as the more important of the two events.

And there are two reasons why. Their names are Richard Petty and David Pearson.

Pearson and Petty. Petty and Pearson. The order of the names depends on your perspective. Both were multiple champions (Petty seven, Pearson three). Both won the series' biggest races. Both were masters at strategy and late-race driving skills. Both had career wins totaling in the triple-digits (Petty won 200, Pearson won 105), the only Sprint Cup drivers to do so.

And in their glory days, they seldom were separated on track. They finished one-two in Cup races a remarkable 63 times.

They were the giants of the sport at the opening of the 1976 season, and the Daytona 500 of that year would bring them together in the most remarkable of ways. Petty was driving the bright red and blue STP-stamped No. 43 that he raced virtually all of his career. Pearson was in the maroon and white, gold-numbered

21 of the Wood Brothers, the car that carried him to what often seemed to be superspeedway invincibility.

It came as no surprise that the 500 of that season rolled to a close with Petty and Pearson racing each other for the victory. It was that way in many other superspeedway races, as pretenders fell by the wayside and the two greats were left to wrestle at the front for the big money.

On this day, the wrestling would be big, indeed.

No one in the packed grandstands knew what to expect, and they got something that probably none of them could have anticipated. And few of them who were there have ever forgotten.

Both Petty and Pearson were respected throughout their careers as smart drivers who didn't often employ hard knocks. They seldom engaged in on-track fender-banging with rivals, and Pearson in particular was remarkable in his ability to avoid accidents.

Considering all that, the events on the last lap of the 1976 500 were stunning.

The two drivers whipped out of the fourth turn the final time nearly side by side with Pearson in front. Petty barely clipped Pearson's car as they began the last run toward the finish line.

That sent both cars spinning into the wall. Petty's car bounced off the wall and slid down the frontstretch, its front-end bashed. Initially, it appeared he might slide all the way across the line and win his sport's biggest race in the wildest way imaginable.

Instead, both cars fell off the banking and onto the grass separating the track from pit road. Pearson, whose Mercury also was crumpled, had the presence of mind as his car spun to depress the clutch, keeping the engine fired. He remained calm on his team radio, asking team mechanic Eddie Wood where Petty's car had landed.

As Petty frantically tried to restart his stalled car, Pearson motored across the finish line at 30-40 mph to win the Daytona

500. It was a finish so wild and unexpected that Hollywood script-writers would have been embarrassed to produce it.

In the aftermath, Pearson said Petty hit him, and Petty admitted it. It wasn't an intentional effort by one driver to crash another, however; it was a competition accident that occurred simply because two determined drivers were chasing the same space.

That those two drivers happened to be the best of their era was just a bonus.

It was great television for ABC, which televised the closing portion of the race live. Also on ABC's sports schedule that day was coverage of the Winter Olympics from Innsbruck, Austria. The network planned to leave the Daytona coverage shortly after the race's end to switch to the Olympics, but the drama in Daytona changed those plans.

"We stayed with the race and ran over several minutes into the Olympics' time," said Dennis Lewin, then an ABC coordinating producer.

It seemed to be the thing to do. After all, two giants were battling.

10 Night Time, Right Time

There are three race tickets that typically bring spreading smiles to fans' faces when they're passed across the sales counter or when they arrive in the mail—the Daytona 500, the Sprint All-Star Race at Charlotte, and the night race at Bristol Motor Speedway in late summer.

A fan vote once tabbed the Bristol night race as the series' most popular.

It certainly should be on the bucket list of every race fan. Even if the race happens to be a little less exciting than anticipated, the experience of being at BMS is worth the price.

The track opened in 1961 on property that had been a dairy farm and was a relatively nondescript half-mile facility tucked away in the mountains of eastern Tennessee, near the Virginia line. Less than 10,000 fans attended some of its early races.

In 1969, track owners decided to renovate the track, and the changes were some of the most dramatic in NASCAR history. The track's 22-degree banking was increased to 36 degrees, the most severe in NASCAR. The immediate effect was to create a racing "bowl," a super-fast half-mile that would push drivers to sensational speeds for a short track.

There was impressive evidence of the track change. On the flatter track, before the renovations, Bobby Isaac won the pole with a speed of 88.669 mph. In the first race after the changes, Cale Yarborough won the pole with a lap of 103.432 mph.

In 1978, the track's August Cup race was moved from afternoon to night, creating an entirely new racing environment and boosting interest in the event.

"We wanted something cool for the fans, cooler on the drivers, and something that would be a different spectacle," said Lanny Hester, then the track's co-owner. "We thought the night race would be a concept we could promote."

He was right. The change was embraced by fans, and attendance for the first night version of the race doubled over the previous season.

"Forty-five minutes into the race, we were still turning cars around and sending them home," said Ed Clark, then public relations director at Bristol and later president of Atlanta Motor Speedway. "So the night thing made it kind of special. There's something special about coming to the mountains that time of year.

I don't know what it is, but it's turned into much more than a race. It's a cult happening."

Television sent the images of tight, fast racing on the Bristol high banks across the country, fueling even more interest, and BMS became one of the hottest tickets in motorsports.

Bristol at night is a witch's brew of exciting possibilities. It's theater in the round on a grand scale with drivers racing so fast and so close together that chaos and mayhem are never surprising. And the sight of a half-mile track with seats reaching to the sky flooded in lights for night racing is a sight in itself.

In the 1990s, new track owner Bruton Smith, who bought the facility in 1996, started a major building program, ultimately increasing the seating capacity to 160,000. Smith literally moved a mountain to accomplish his goals, knocking down an area near the grandstands to even out the property and allow for seating additions. Over four winters, the track added 118,000 seats.

Before tough economic years hampered ticket sales, Bristol put together a streak of 55 straight sellouts.

11 On the Wing

Few NASCAR race cars have produced a level of excitement and drama equal to that of the so-called winged racers of the late 1960s and early 1970s.

The cars were beauties. They had long sleek noses and—more importantly—rear-deck wings that rose high into the air. Watching them race two- and three-abreast in the draft at Talladega Superspeedway was a dynamic sight.

But you had to watch quickly to see it. The winged-car era in NASCAR racing lasted less than two years.

The concept began at Chrysler, where Dodge engineers, working on the Charger to better its competition profile, made the nose sharper and lower and tacked on the rear wing. Looking at the new model—the Dodge Daytona—for the first time, some observers said it looked like a "car" from the *Jetsons*, a cartoon show about a futuristic family.

Indeed, it was the future of racing.

Chrysler built a nearly identical Plymouth model—the Superbird. In testing, the new cars set record speeds at Daytona and Talladega, and there was intense interest in how they would perform in the inaugural Talladega 500 on the brand new Alabama International Motor Speedway (now Talladega Superspeedway) in September 1969. The drama was blunted, however, when the new track was too fast for the tire technology of the day, and most of the leading drivers boycotted the race.

A Dodge Daytona driven by Richard Brickhouse won the 500.

The winged cars ran the rest of that season, and Superbird driver Pete Hamilton gave them a very important victory in the 1970 Daytona 500 while driving for Petty Enterprises.

A month later, Buddy Baker became the first stock car driver to run 200 mph on a closed course when he hit 200.096 mph in a Cotton Owens–prepared Dodge Daytona at Talladega. Later in the session, he boosted the speed to 200.447 mph.

Harry Hyde, who was crew chief for driver Bobby Isaac during the winged-car period, later called them "almost the perfect race car." He said a slight tilting of the deck wing could control the car's handling in banking.

In fact, the biggest problem with the winged cars is that they were too good. As speeds climbed, NASCAR officials got nervous. The officials required the use of carburetor restrictor plates at Michigan International Speedway in August 1970.

Then NASCAR developed rules for the 1971 season that limited the engine size in the specialty cars, thus removing their advantage. That basically wrote "finish" to the cars' history at the top level of stock car racing.

12 Jeff Gordon

He roared into NASCAR racing with the promise of greatness—and with a hurriedly grown mustache to make him look older.

Jeff Gordon made his debut in Sprint Cup racing in 1992, a whiz kid from California who had dominated every type of motorsports he had tried and who also figured to shake up the NASCAR world. He was a new sort of driver for NASCAR, an open-wheel-trained youngster who wasn't from the South, didn't carry the hardscrabble background of many who had conquered stock car racing, and brought along Hollywood good looks and personality. His sort had never been seen in Cup racing, but it didn't take him long to make himself known.

Former Charlotte Motor Speedway president Humpy Wheeler, an excellent judge of racing talent, introduced Gordon to the stock car world when Gordon was 20. "I've seen a lot of drivers in my 30-odd years in racing," Wheeler said. "You have rare people come into a sport—like [Muhammad] Ali when he came into boxing, Arnold Palmer into golf, A.J. Foyt and Richard Petty in racing—guys that just come along once every quarter-century or decade or whatever. And Jeff Gordon may be the finest young racing talent in the world today. I think you're going to hear a lot of noise from this guy. He's a rare talent."

Jeff Gordon prepares to take to the track for the AAA 400 qualifying session on October 1, 2011, at the Dover International Speedway in Dover, Delaware.
(Cal Sport Media via AP Images)

Gordon stood beside Wheeler, looking much younger than his 20 years. In fact, he looked very much like a bagboy from the local supermarket.

Gordon made his Sprint Cup debut in the final race of the 1992 season, driving a Chevrolet for his new boss, Rick Hendrick. Ironically, that event—the Hooters 500 at Atlanta Motor Speedway—also was the last race in Richard Petty's driving career. As one superstar left, another potential star arrived.

Although Gordon seemed amazingly young, his racing career was actually 15 years old. His stepfather, John Bickford, bought Gordon a quarter-midget race car when he was 5 years old, and Gordon competed at tracks near the family's Vallejo, California, home. Gordon won his first quarter-midget championship when he was 8 years old and while racing against drivers twice his age.

Bickford recognized his stepson's potential, and in 1986, the family moved to Pittsboro, Indiana, to be closer to more racetracks and so Gordon could race against adults, something he couldn't do in California because of age restrictions. It was a calculated gamble that paid off big-time.

Gordon joined the United States Auto Club at 16, becoming the youngest person to get a license from the organization. He won three Sprint Car track championships before he was old enough to get a driver's license, and in 1989, he was the USAC Midget Rookie of the Year.

On the evening of his graduation from Tri-West High School in Lizton, Indiana, Gordon raced in a dirt-track event in Bloomington, Indiana.

Gordon won the USAC Midget championship in 1990, then moved up to the bigger Silver Crown cars the next season and also won that title. After that accomplishment, Bickford sent Gordon to the Buck Baker Driving School in Rockingham, North Carolina, to give him a taste of driving NASCAR stock cars. It was almost time for Gordon to make a crossroads decision—continue along the road to racing open-wheel cars or detour to NASCAR.

On his first day at the Buck Baker Driving School, Gordon said he knew stock cars were for him. He jumped into the then Busch Series in 1991, winning Rookie of the Year. In 1992, he won 11 pole positions in the series and attracted the attention of Hendrick, who signed Gordon to a contract to race at NASCAR's highest level, convinced that Gordon had the right stuff.

"A talent like Jeff does not come along very often," Hendrick said. "We didn't have it in our long-range plan to add another team, but Jeff made the decision for us. We feel he is NASCAR's next superstar."

The rest of Gordon's story has been the stuff of legend. He scored his first Cup point win in dramatic fashion in the 1994 Coca-Cola 600 at Charlotte, and he followed that with one of the biggest triumphs in NASCAR history as he won the inaugural Brickyard 400 at Indianapolis Motor Speedway in his adopted home state. He quickly picked up the nickname "Wonder Boy."

The Indianapolis win, scored in front of 300,000 at the world's most famous racetrack, shot Gordon's career into orbit. "When we got back to the office the Tuesday after Indy, the desk was covered up [with telephone messages], and the phone hasn't stopped ringing since," said Ron Miller, Gordon's longtime public relations chief.

Gordon's first Cup championship followed in 1995. Working with crew chief Ray Evernham, he also won titles in 1997 and 1998 as his team put together—from 1996 to 1998—a remarkable run in which he won a total of 33 races.

Among those praising Gordon as he moved through race fields with ease was Petty, the driver who set the standard for Cup victories with 200. "He's in the very top three or four that's ever been here," Petty said. "That's just because he understands what's going on. He's a real versatile driver. He takes whatever circumstances are thrown at him and makes the best of it. Everybody can't do that.

"He doesn't seem to get rattled when they have problems. He's pretty level-headed. He understands what it takes for the car and for him."

Gordon quickly built a reputation as the top driver of his era. He was fast, smart, and fearless.

In the 1997 Daytona 500, Gordon made one of the most outrageous passes in the history of the sport to win its biggest race. Late in the race, Gordon drove deep to the inside in the first turn and made his car stick, passing leader Bill Elliott in what was basically a new passing lane Gordon created. He won the race under caution.

In 1999, Gordon made a similar pass of Rusty Wallace in the same area of the track to win that year's Daytona 500. Two bold moves and two wins in NASCAR's marquee event. Those races helped define Gordon as the star driver of the 1990s, and veteran observers began ranking him with the top drivers of all time.

He also took the sport into new territories, appearing on the cover of non-sports magazines, hosting *Saturday Night Live,* and making several appearances on other nationally televised programs. He was lightning caught in a bottle.

Through it all, Gordon has been the cooperative superstar. He is highly respected among the NASCAR news media, which seeks his opinion on every issue of the day. His foundation raises millions for children's hospitals, and he is a favorite driver of the Make-A-Wish Foundation. Despite intense demands on his schedule, he tries to make time for young fans.

"I try to be a role model and let them see that at this level you still can be someone who has a positive effect on the people you meet and take time for them," he said. "I'm not better than anybody else. I've just reached a certain level with a certain ability I have, and that puts me in the public eye. So I try to put myself in the place of people who are interested in what I'm doing."

13 Dale Earnhardt Jr.

Even considering the money, the prestige, the ability to hang with other superstars, and having someone to handle the worrisome gnats of life, it isn't easy being Dale Earnhardt Jr.

Imagine being John Wayne Jr. or Elvis Presley Jr. or Michael Jordan Jr. This is the place where Dale Jr. resides. He carries one of the most famous names in motorsports history, and he also rides daily with an unmatched legacy.

Not only did Dale Earnhardt Sr. win races (76) and championships (seven) with seeming ease, but he also had a personality that was a perfect match for the majority of the fan base of his era. He was all country. He hunted. He fished. He listened to country music. He grew up on a Southern textile village "mill hill." He was everything a Johnny Reb wanted in a hero.

When Dale Sr. died, the sport of stock car racing underwent a schism of sorts. Some longtime fans, stunned by the loss of The Man, left the sport entirely. In one case, a fan took this concept to the extreme. After Earnhardt died, thousands of fans left memorabilia—caps, photos, T-shirts, etc.—along a fence at Earnhardt's race shop in Mooresville, North Carolina. One man left his prosthetic leg with a note explaining that he wouldn't be needing it because, with Earnhardt gone, he wouldn't be going to races.

Other fans wandered in the wilderness, in search of another driver they could follow. But a significant group of Senior's former disciples immediately lined up behind Dale Jr., figuring the son also rises.

So Junior, who began his Sprint Cup career in 1999, two years before his father's death, almost immediately became the hope of thousands of fans. He had his own followers—attracted to his

Dale Earnhardt Jr. shares a laugh while preparing for the Irwin Tools Night Race on Saturday, August 26, 2011, in Bristol, Tennessee. (AP Photo/ Lisa Norman-Hudson)

youth, his talent, his looks—and now many of his father's fans arrived, trading one Earnhardt for another.

Junior is his father's son, but there are significant differences between them. Junior is into computers and video games—two things his father shunned, and Junior's musical tastes are quite the opposite of his dad's. Although proud of his North Carolina roots, Junior isn't aggressively "country."

Being Junior occasionally seems to wear on Earnhardt. To be the son of one of the sport's greatest racers is to be subjected to overblown expectations, particularly in recent years as he has struggled to reach victory lane. The Earnhardt family seal has seemed to be a heavy burden during that stretch.

But Junior wanted to race from a very early age. There is no turning back.

"I asked to be in this position," he said. "I wanted to be a race car driver, and I have a famous last name, and that goes with the territory.

"Sometimes you get kind of worn down. You get tired of trying to explain what happened. When things go bad, you don't really feel like trying to sit in front of everybody and try to tell them why it went bad and what you might be trying to do to make it not go bad any more. But I dug that pit, and I've got to lie in it, I guess. Somehow or other, you sort of recharge your batteries."

Earnhardt Jr. said he remembered taking heat from school classmates when Dale Sr. raced. "When Bobby Allison's tire blew at Talladega [in 1987] and he hit the wall [and almost landed in the grandstand], some kid blamed my dad for that," he said. "My dad was running about five car lengths behind Bobby. Some kid the next day at school was trying to tell me how my dad almost killed somebody. That was his exact quote.

"That to me was normal. That was life. That was how things were. You dealt with it, and it was all right."

Now Junior, having relocated to Hendrick Motorsports after leaving Dale Earnhardt Inc., the team his father started, drives into the future, carrying his name, his dad's name, and everything that goes with them.

14 Dale Inman: That "Other" Dale

Fans tend to get excited about the big championship numbers all-time greats Richard Petty and Dale Earnhardt Sr. rang up. And rightly so.

Petty won Cup championships in 1964, '67, '71, '72, '74, '75 and '79. Earnhardt matched that total of seven with titles in '80, '86, '87, '90, '91, '93 and '94.

Petty is retired, and Earnhardt was killed in the 2001 Daytona 500. They will stay tied at seven titles, a NASCAR record. But shouldn't there be a shout out for a guy with *eight* Cup championships?

That would be Dale Inman, who was crew chief for all seven of Petty's championships—plus the 1984 title won by Terry Labonte.

Inman and Petty were first cousins and grew up riding bicycles and playing along the backroads of Level Cross, North Carolina, then home to the Petty Enterprises race shop. It seemed only natural that when Richard followed his father, Lee, into racing that Inman would follow Richard.

They became a potent team, with Richard quickly showing the driving talent linked to the Petty name and Inman developing ways and means to make the Petty cars faster and faster. Inman, along with Wood Brothers Racing crew chief Leonard Wood, is given credit by many for developing the template for the modern crew chief.

Inman, now officially retired from racing but still a frequent traveler and consultant with the Richard Petty Motorsports operation, was exceptional at making the correct pit calls at critical times. Change two tires? Four? None? Stretch the fuel an extra lap? Inman was rarely wrong with such decisions.

Some of the choices were gambles, and Inman won most of those. In the 1981 Daytona 500, he brought Petty into the pits late for a quick splash-and-go stop, electing not to change tires with more than 20 laps to go. The tires held for the closing miles, giving Petty his seventh 500 victory.

Inman cried in victory lane after that win, and it turned out he was keeping a secret. He left the Pettys a few weeks later to work for another team and eventually won the eighth championship with Labonte in 1984. He returned to the Petty team as a manager in 1986.

Inman often kids Petty about being ahead of him in the championship count.

When Inman was elected to the 2012 NASCAR Hall of Fame class (Petty was part of the first class in 2010), Petty came over to congratulate him. "I told him that I should have gone in before him; I've got eight championships," Inman said with a smile.

15 Jimmie Johnson

When Jimmie Johnson virtually took over the Sprint Cup Series in the 2000s, the question popped to the surface: Could this bright and talented guy from California be NASCAR's best driver ever?

He certainly put forth a sparkling resume—championship after championship after championship, forming a string of titles that first passed Cale Yarborough's former record of three straight and then shot Johnson into an orbit of its own with four in a row—and then a fifth.

Observers began talking about Johnson, who dropped into Cup racing after a background in off-road trucks and stadium truck racing, in the same breath as Richard Petty, David Pearson, Cale Yarborough, Dale Earnhardt Sr., Jeff Gordon, and some of the sport's other greats.

Petty, the sport's all-time victory leader with 200 and owner of the championship trophy record of seven (along with Earnhardt), isn't a fan of comparing drivers from different eras because of the obvious equipment and style differences that divide the years, but Johnson's extended run certainly grabbed Petty's attention. "There was an era that I kind of dominated," Petty said. "There was an era there that Earnhardt dominated. There was an era that Jeff Gordon dominated. This is Jimmie Johnson's era. That's about the only way to compare it.

"You can't compare apples and oranges, and that's what you try to do if you take what he's done and try to put it in perspective with what other people have done. You really can't do that.

"There was David Pearson's time, Bobby Allison's time, Cale Yarborough's time, Petty's time. Right now it's Jimmie's time."

Mark Martin, who sought titles even as he watched Johnson claim them, said the true merit of what Johnson has accomplished over recent seasons won't be appreciated for some time. "I think everyone has it tempered some," Martin said. "I don't think that they really realize that they're getting their brains beat in by that group like they really are in today's age. I think when we get 10, 20 years down the road and look back, people will realize what an incredible feat that they have achieved.

"Golly, who would expect that to discontinue any time soon based on what you see? Incredible, incredible stuff that they're doing and have done."

Jimmie Johnson climbs into his car before practice for the race at Charlotte Motor Speedway in Concord, North Carolina, on Friday, October 14, 2011.
(AP Photo/Rick Havner)

Arriving in Sprint Cup racing from a largely undistinguished run in the Busch (now Nationwide) Series, Johnson has been a perpetual motion machine at stock car racing's top level. With the early advocacy of Gordon, who convinced team owner Rick Hendrick to hire Johnson and then watched as Johnson's star rose while Gordon lost some sparkle, Johnson found his place quickly.

Johnson's ride has been punishing and frustrating for the opposition. "You go home some nights and think, 'Man, I should just get a job at the 7-Eleven,'" Steve Hmiel, director of competition at Earnhardt Ganassi Racing, said. "What they've done is actually fantastic. They've taken pretty close to the same amount of horsepower [as everyone else], pretty close to the same amount of downforce, pretty close to the same amount of pit stop times, the same systems, and they've whipped us."

Hmiel, a longtime roamer of pit road in various positions, stopped short of saying Johnson's series of championships trumps the title runs of Petty and Earnhardt. "It's incredible, but it's a different kind of incredible," Hmiel said. "In the '70s, we raced everywhere, and we didn't have the support systems at home getting things done while we weren't there. We didn't have the computers. Now, that hasn't made their job easier. It's made their job different. Everybody else has computers and support systems at home, too.

"Back then, it was different because it was more about the group of guys who went off and raced their guts out and kind of reacted to the moment. That's what I think was so great about the Petty Enterprises teams and the Junior Johnson teams and those guys. They reacted to the moment. You didn't have a long-range plan."

Rusty Wallace, who won the Sprint Cup championship in 1989, voiced similar views in comparing the past and present. "I'm a little old school," Wallace said. "I don't think I'll ever be able to put anybody in the same class with Earnhardt and Petty. But to think about Jimmie Johnson and what he's done is totally amazing. The numbers are startling. But it's two different eras. Earnhardt and the stuff he accomplished on the racetrack, the aggressive, wild driving. And Petty, back in the old days, getting it all started—all that still holds a special place in my heart.

"This is really important what Jimmie is doing, but the sport is more technical now. Back then it was more raw, more brute force. Now it's all technical. And the technical stuff is something that Johnson and the Hendrick teams have been fantastic at. All these engineers, all these amazing amounts of people. Still, everybody is in the same ballpark and has the same opportunity."

Carl Edwards described Johnson and the No. 48 team as "that team that won't go away. They don't ever lie down. When they're not great, they're good. They're never bad. And that's what I think makes them so tough."

The idea—supported here and there—that Johnson is a minor component in the overall Hendrick success, or that virtually anyone could have driven the 48 cars to a string of titles—is rebuffed by series veterans.

"I listen to Jimmie over the radio," said Jimmy Makar, Joe Gibbs Racing senior vice president of racing operations. "I watch what he does on the racetrack. Jimmie Johnson is a student of the sport. He's looking at it and studying it all the time.

"You just listen to him and watch what he does. I think he's different from a lot of people in that. He has impressed me in the way he's gone about trying to win races and get better over time."

Former Cup champion Dale Jarrett said he is amazed that Johnson's accomplishments haven't gained more respect and admiration.

"I don't think he gets the accolades he should," Jarrett said. "He works out extremely hard. He keeps himself in great physical condition. He thinks about this constantly. He's given up a lot to get to this point.

"I think the perception is because he has the best cars and the best team and the best crew chief in the business then why shouldn't he win? But we've seen other drivers with a lot of talent put in that position who couldn't get the job done."

16 A Call to the Hall

Glory Road is exactly that. The highlight of the new NASCAR Hall of Fame, located in Charlotte, North Carolina, is a changing collection of 18 notable race cars from the beginnings of NASCAR through the modern era.

The cars are lined up in order of age along a sweeping arc inside the Great Hall of the Hall of Fame building. The road that contains the cars increases in banking to illustrate the fact that NASCAR events have been held on surfaces ranging from flat tracks to steep banks.

The Hall, a dream of NASCAR executives for years, opened May 11, 2010. Its main purpose is to honor individuals who have impacted NASCAR at high levels, and those Hall members are spotlighted in the Hall of Honor in the central section of the new building. But the Hall of Fame is much more than a place to identify stock car racing's best. It also is a repository for a treasure trove of racing memorabilia, a place to explain the sport's past and to explore its future, and a home to an array of interactive exhibits.

Although NASCAR drivers, team owners, mechanics, and officials have been honored by being named to any number of other halls of fame (some motorsports related, some not), the NASCAR Hall automatically became the most prestigious of the group when it inducted its first-year class of Richard Petty, Bill France Sr., Dale Earnhardt Sr., Junior Johnson, and Bill France Jr.

Artifacts related to the first five inductees were on display in the Hall of Honor for a year. Then the "spires," the tall metal pieces explaining the accomplishments of each member, were moved to an outside ring around the Hall of Honor to make way for artifacts for the second hall class. That change will take place every year as five new members are elected to the hall.

Beyond the Hall of Honor and Glory Road, the building houses case after case of racing artifacts from 60-year-old trophies and other awards to driver uniforms, battered race helmets, presidential mementos presented to drivers, unique tools, and unusual photographs.

A racing simulator area provides one of the best virtual racing experiences available. Visitors can perform pit stops, walk through a team transporter, and visit a "shop" area that illustrates how teams prepare cars to go to the track.

The hall also includes a theater that shows a short film providing an overview of NASCAR.

17 Herb Thomas

One of the best drivers of NASCAR's pioneer years—Herb Thomas—stepped into NASCAR racing from farm fields. Thomas was a corn and tobacco farmer in rural North Carolina. There was no reason to expect that he would ever be anything else. He had no connections to racing or fast cars.

But all that changed when Thomas attended a Modified race in Greensboro, North Carolina, in the late 1940s, when motorsports in the South was still trying to find its balance. It was a good race that night, good enough to catch the attention of Thomas. He watched the cars circle the track at high speed and the drivers move in and out of traffic, and he caught the fever.

"I went to Greensboro to see a race and figured if they could do it, I could, too," Thomas said. "It was something I liked to do. I got to beat somebody else."

It was that simple for Thomas. He was a self-made man, and he had no doubts that he could make things happen in race cars. So he set about doing it.

Thomas entered the first Cup (then Strictly Stock) race in Charlotte in 1949 and soon showed his skills. He became the series' first two-time champion (in 1951 and 1953) and also was the first driver to win the storied Southern 500, one of NASCAR's most difficult races, three times (1951, '54, and '55).

Those were different days. Drivers often drove their street cars to tracks and then raced them. "I remember playing the radio in a race car," Thomas said. "I raced at a track up in New York where the dust was so thick all you could see was the tops of trees at each end of the track. You looked for the trees, then turned. Then you'd go to the other end, look for the trees and make a turn."

For Thomas, racing was that simple. There wasn't anything excessively complicated about it. He got in a car, figured out how to make it go fast, and chased people down. And he won.

Thomas took 48 checkered flags before crash injuries essentially ended his career in 1962. He attended a few races in later years but was a quiet man who seldom talked about his driving days.

After his racing career ended, Thomas returned to farming and later operated a trucking company.

18 Martinsville Speedway

Compared to most of the other racetracks in NASCAR, Martinsville Speedway looks like it would be a snap for some of the world's best drivers. It's the Sprint Cup circuit's shortest and slowest oval. From above, it looks like a paper clip—two straights connected by a couple of tight turns.

Not much of a challenge, right? Wrong.

Martinsville remains one of the tour's toughest tracks to conquer. Even a driver with a resume as strong as Hall of Famer Bobby Allison couldn't put his name on the Martinsville winners list.

Martinsville is basically flat, banked only 12 degrees in the turns. The straightaways are only 800' long. You drive fast down the straight, turn left, then do it again. Five hundred laps. One thousand left turns.

It's a long day, but it's a short track, one generally similar to the sort that almost every driver grows up on. Why then is it so hard to conquer?

"I had never competed on a track that was so tight with the radii of the corners and the long straightaways," said Jimmie Johnson, a multiple winner at Martinsville. "I'm glad that we didn't because I was really tough on the brakes coming up through the ranks and trying to learn how to drive a stock car. I don't think I would have made 500 laps in my early days. This track demands a lot out of the car and the driver, and patience is a big part of that.

"Your mental discipline inside the car—there are a lot of guys that are fast in the beginning of the race or the middle part of the race and can get frustrated easily with traffic and make bad decisions. If you have a bad pit stop, it is easy to lose your cool and it is real difficult to pass cars. A driver has a lot on his hands here to keep his head in the game. Also, there is a lot of weight on the pit crews because if you do have a bad stop and you do lose a lot of track position, it's tough to get back in contention and get to where you were when you started."

Drivers must attack but also must know the limits. Being too aggressive can eat brakes and waste cars for the final hundred laps. Taking it too easy can result in falling off the lead lap.

"You can't tiptoe around the race track," Johnson said. "There are certain areas where you really have to attack to turn a fast lap, and they don't come natural for the majority of the drivers. It took me a few trips, and I was in a position where I was being lapped by the race leader, who was Tony Stewart at the time. To follow him and visually see where he was attacking, I had it all wrong.

"We've all talked about it, but there is a certain rhythm that the track requires for you to run a fast lap time. And on top of that, a fast lap time is maybe a tenth of a second better than a slow one. So there are really, really small adjustments that you have to make."

Brakes always are an issue at Martinsville, and driver Greg Biffle said braking technique is critical.

"There is a lot of technique to the brake, when you brake, coming off the corner," Biffle said. "If the car doesn't have bite with the front tires and won't stop straight and wants to pull hard to the left or slide that left front tire—if the car won't do those things, then there is nothing the driver can do to mask them because the speed is so slow. We can't arc it out and get a different angle because the speed is so slow. If that car won't do its thing, then you don't stand a chance."

And that's exactly where some very good drivers stand at Martinsville.

During NASCAR's big growth spurt in the 1990s, as attendance totals and television ratings grew, there was talk that the sport had raced past places like Martinsville Speedway. Shut them down and move on, the chatter went. We've got bigger fish to fry. Track president Clay Campbell seemed to be constantly on the defensive, beating back talk that his speedway would lose one—maybe both—of its Cup dates.

But NASCAR has committed to continuing to run at its oldest Cup track for the foreseeable future, and that means continuing memories of the three most notable non-racers who roamed the old speedway grounds—founder H. Clay Earles, public relations guru Dick Thompson, and public address announcer H. Lewis Compton.

Earles was old-line NASCAR through and through. Full of himself and full of stories—some of them printable—that stretched back to pre-NASCAR days, he was a mainstay at the track even in his twilight years, and garage-area residents were never really sure if he still carried that pistol with which he enforced rules and regulations early on.

Thompson largely invented the role of speedway public relations director in early NASCAR and knew more about the sport than virtually any five other people. He could not have imagined the Facebook and Twitter era, but in his time, no one did it better.

Compton was the template for the old-time Southern speedway announcer, his dulcet tones floating over the track and often above the engine roar. He had no script. He was often at his most entertaining when he'd spot children playing too close to the track fence and would suddenly get louder on the microphone: "Hey, you kids by the Turn 4 fence! Get away from there!"

That's Martinsville.

19 Five That Race the Heart

The NASCAR Sprint Cup Series has one of the sports world's longest seasons, stretching from early February to mid-November. Its schedule bounces from the Northeast to southern California and from the southern tip of Florida to the heart of the Midwest.

The 36-race schedule (plus two special events that are not included in the seasonal point standings) contains huge oval tracks, half-mile short tracks, and a pair of winding road courses. The racing is unique at every stop, although some of the tracks seem almost identical.

Circumstances differ each year, but there are certain races that typically fit into the "can't miss" category, ones that eager fans travel many miles to attend. These events generally offer some of the best racing, fiercest finishes, and biggest fun of the season.

In no particular order:

Daytona 500, Daytona International Speedway, Daytona Beach, Florida—DIS is considered the cathedral of NASCAR racing, and the 500 is the biggest race in all of stock car racing. It opens the schedule, and teams spend much of the off-season fine-tuning cars in search of the 500 checkered flag. The days leading to the race and Daytona 500 day itself make up one of the most intense periods of the season.

Irwin Tools Night Race, Bristol Motor Speedway, Bristol, Tennessee—Bristol, located in the mountains of eastern Tennessee, is NASCAR's top short track. A high-banked cereal bowl of a facility, it produces very high speeds for a half-mile, and trouble often lurks around the next corner. The track's allure produced a sellout streak of more than 50 races.

Southern 500, Darlington Raceway, Darlington, South Carolina—Darlington is NASCAR's oldest major track. Opened in 1950, it retains much of the atmosphere that has welcomed competitors and fans for more than six decades. Considered the Fenway Park of stock car racing, its oblong shape and tight racing are unique in the sport.

The Sprint All-Star Race, Charlotte Motor Speedway, Concord, North Carolina—The annual All-Star race is a non-points event, and that adds to its special nature. Drivers go into the race with no thought of "saving" cars for a long run or simply hoping for a high finish. It's all about winning, and the purse tops $1 million. The night atmosphere makes the race electric.

Talladega 500, Talladega Superspeedway, Talladega, Alabama— Talladega has been the site of some of the most amazing finishes in the history of NASCAR. Its high banks and ultra-fast speeds create vibrant racing that makes it one of stock car racing's capitals, and its fall race is enhanced by being part of the Chase. And the infield is one of racing's most entertaining.

20 Bud Moore: A True American Hero

In auto racing, there are heroes, and then there are *heroes*. Bud Moore fits firmly in the latter category. He won Sprint Cup championships as a car owner and crew chief. He won the Daytona 500 as a car owner. He also was on the ground for NASCAR's raw beginnings.

But the bigger story of Walter "Bud" Moore's life revolves around the unusual heroism he displayed as a South Carolina

NASCAR Hall of Famer Bud Moore stands next to Ryan Newman's car on pit row before the qualifying laps for the Heluva Good! Sour Cream Dips 400 at Michigan International Speedway in Brooklyn, Michigan, on Saturday, June 18, 2011. (AP Photo/Bob Brodbeck)

teenager thrust into some of the fiercest fighting in World War II. Moore's racing exploits—and, not incidentally, his bravery in war—earned him NASCAR's highest honor—a place in the NASCAR Hall of Fame. He was inducted in 2011.

One of 10 children growing up on a Carolina farm, Moore began tinkering with fast cars as a teenager. His farm life was interrupted at the age of 18 when he was drafted into the army at the peak of World War II.

A year later, in June 1944, he was in one of the first army units that hit the beaches of Normandy as the United States and its allies began the march that reclaimed Europe from the Nazis. Moore and another soldier captured 15 German soldiers and four officers during the Battle of the Bulge. Moore, later promoted to sergeant, was wounded five times and received numerous medals.

"We had a job to do, and a lot of good men died doing it," Moore said.

After the war, he returned home to Spartanburg, South Carolina, and jumped with both feet into the postwar automobile craze that swept the country. He and a Spartanburg friend, Joe Eubanks, quickly became interested in the ragtag sport of stock car racing, which was semi-organized at best in that period. NASCAR was still two years from being formed.

Moore drove a few race cars but slapped the wall a few times and figured he was too big and tall to be a driver, anyway. That eventually led him into a crew chief position in 1950s NASCAR and to the top of the sport, then into team ownership.

Moore won his first championship as crew chief for Buck Baker in 1957.

Moore found early team-owner success with the talented Joe Weatherly, as the former motorcycle racer won championships in 1962 and 1963, but Moore also was hit in the heart by the dangers

A Moonlit Night

Over the course of several decades in racing, Bud Moore matched wits with legendary racer/mechanic/car owner Junior Johnson on many occasions. Moore won some, and he lost some. But he never really rallied from a particularly eventful encounter with Johnson, one he remembers too vividly:

"We were coming back from a Richmond race one year and ran up on Junior Johnson and his guys," Moore said. "They saw us coming and kept holding us up. Wouldn't let us by. Finally, they pulled over to the left side to let us by. We got up beside them, and I was ready to shake my fist at them.

"Then I saw Junior. Stuck his big rump out the window. Mooned us. I couldn't believe it."

It was a different side of Johnson, one Moore doesn't want to experience again.

associated with the business. Weatherly was killed in a brutal accident on the Riverside, California, road course in January 1964. A year later, during a tire test at Daytona International Speedway, Billy Wade, also driving for Moore, died when his right front tire blew and sent his car hurtling into the first-turn wall.

Moore drove home and told his wife, Betty, that he didn't think he could race anymore. But he returned and worked on safety advances that addressed the brake problem that apparently led to Weatherly's crash and the seat harness issue that was a factor in Wade's sudden death.

Moore built a strong relationship with Ford Motor Co. officials and raced the company's cars for most of his career. In the late 1960s, he detoured from NASCAR at the request of the car builder to run its Trans-Am Series road-racing operation.

He found success there, also, winning the series championship in 1970 with driver Parnelli Jones piloting the Moore Mustangs. Dan Gurney and David Pearson also drove Moore's Trans-Am cars. One of those Mustangs, restored to its racing glory, sold a few years ago at a collector-car auction for $343,000.

Moore's racing career put him in at least one really bad spot.

Before repeated problems on pit road led NASCAR to call for speed limits for pit-road traffic, team members routinely stepped onto the pit surface to hold signs so that their drivers could readily identify their pit location as they roared in at amazingly fast speeds. Now this is done safely with signs that hang on poles, but then team members did the work "up close and personal."

Moore assigned that job to himself for many years. During the Coca-Cola 600 at Charlotte Motor Speedway, his driver, Brett Bodine, slid through his pit when his car hit a wet surface, and it slammed into Moore, tossing him into the pit wall.

"I told him [via the team radio] to take it easy coming in because somebody had spilled something in the pit next to ours," Moore said. "He was coming in pretty hot. When he got on the brakes real hard, the car got sort of sideways straight into me. I jumped straight up and landed on the hood, and it threw me into the air and onto pit wall.

"They finished the pit stop and got him out of there. It broke my right leg and tore ligaments in my knee."

Moore's final words to Bodine (who now drives the pace car on NASCAR weekends) on the radio as they hauled him away on a stretcher: "Boy, you better win this damn race."

By the way, Bodine did not.

Moore sold his Sprint Cup team in 1999 and retired from NASCAR racing to return to farming. He owns a huge cattle farm near Spartanburg.

21 Wendell Scott

Every NASCAR independent driver—defined as those who race against the wind with limited resources and virtually no sponsorship—faces a hard road. None, though, had a rougher ride than Wendell Scott, who raced at NASCAR's top level from 1961 to 1973.

Scott was a short-track driving champion from Virginia. He was a mechanical whiz, having served as a mechanic in the army during World War II. He prepared, worked on, and repaired his own race cars.

And he was black. Although modern-day NASCAR has made strides toward diversifying its landscape, during the years that Scott competed on the Cup circuit, the environment for a black driver was difficult at best and hostile at worst.

Scott was banned from several speedways—including NASCAR's oldest big track, Darlington Raceway—simply because of his color. He did not stir the waters. He went on the road trying to fulfill a passion for speed, and he wanted to race on the high ground of the sport along with the Pettys, Pearsons, and Allisons. Yet his race sometimes denied him entry into the event.

The NASCAR trip also was difficult on Scott's family, which typically made up his crew. They were not welcome at many restaurants and hotels along the racing trail, so they often had to drive long distances out of the way to find places to stay, and they had more than a few picnics of sandwiches and potato chips because they couldn't share a meal in a restaurant.

Yet Scott persevered. He maintained his racing operation by winning enough money to keep his cars moving, and he received

A First for Joie Ray

Although Wendell Scott scored the first victory by a black driver in NASCAR history, he was not the first African-American to take the track. That honor went to Joie Ray, who drove a Henry J to finish 51st (in a field of 61 cars) in a race on the Daytona beach-road course in 1952.

assistance with parts and pieces now and then from fellow racers, most of whom were much more accepting of him than the general public appeared to be.

The struggle paid off for Scott on December 1, 1963, at Jacksonville, Florida. On that day, Scott's Chevrolet was one of the strongest cars in the field on the half-mile dirt Speedway Park track, and at the end of the day, he took the checkered flag.

Even then, however, Scott was a victim of prejudice. Officials, concerned about the problems that might be prompted by a black driver's win (including the drama that might unfold in victory lane if Scott kissed the white trophy queen), announced Buck Baker as the race winner.

Scott, who knew he was the real winner, drove home empty-handed. NASCAR corrected the mistake and presented him with a race trophy at a later date (and he received the $1,000 winner's check), but there was no celebration, and the victory had a hollow tone.

Almost a half-century later, Scott remains the only black driver with a victory in any of NASCAR's major series. Injuries finally forced the end of his driving career in 1973.

Scott died on December 23, 1990, his legacy still an unresolved issue for many. He was not NASCAR's first black driver, but he was the only one to race consistently over a period of several years. There is no denying that he left a profile in courage as a black man who fought back in a sport that was virtually 100 percent white.

In a different era and in better equipment, in the opinion of drivers who raced against him, Scott could have been a top-10 competitor. It was only after his death that his accomplishments—and his struggle—came into clear view.

22 Hot Dog!

On the NASCAR circuit, there is no more anticipated dining delicacy than the Martinsville hot dog. Drivers, crew members, fans, and NASCAR officials wait patiently in line at concession stands to buy the $2 dog. Actually, dogs (plural). No one can eat just one.

In fact, that's the point. On every visit to the tour's oldest track, some team members engage in an unofficial contest to see who can consume the most hot dogs. It is a gastric delight.

The Martinsville dog—it can be served with slaw or chili and onions—has been a staple at the track for many years. It's even sometimes breakfast fare for crewmen who arrive early.

"There's nothing really special about it, other than the fact that you can get everything on it, unlike most stadiums and tracks where you just get the bun and wiener and you have to finish your own," Martinsville Speedway president Clay Campbell said. Campbell's grandfather, Clay Earles, built the track, and it's safe to say the grandson grew up on track dogs.

But these are not just any hot dogs.

The special nature of the Martinsville delicacy was proven in 2004 when International Speedway Corp. bought the track and its Americrown food service arm took over the concessions.

Pit Stops for Provisions

Before virtually every NASCAR driver bought an expensive motorhome to become his home away from home at race tracks, most stayed in hotels in or near that week's race host city. They traveled in the same circles as race fans and ate at the same restaurants.

In fact, a given race city's most popular restaurant often was the best place—other than the race track, obviously—to bump into a race car driver. Now, with the top drivers "living" in the speedway driver-owner compound at most tracks and traveling cooks preparing most—if not all—of their meals, that race-weekend highlight is almost non-existent.

That does not mean, however, that grabbing a bite to eat can't be an adventure on the NASCAR trail. It just so happens that some of the best—or best racing-related—restaurants in the country are located near speedways. If the food isn't great, the atmosphere usually is. And sometimes you get both.

Here's a list of a few that shouldn't be missed if you're in the neighborhood:

- Manhattan's, Griffin, Georgia, near Atlanta Motor Speedway
- Top O' The River, Anniston, Alabama, near Talladega Superspeedway
- Chart House and Stavro's Pizza House, Daytona Beach, Florida, near Daytona International Speedway
- Raceway Grill, Darlington, South Carolina, near Darlington Raceway
- St. Elmo Steak House, Indianapolis, Indiana, near Indianapolis Motor Speedway
- Sambo's Tavern, Dover, Delaware, near Dover International Speedway
- Fiorella's Jack Stack Barbecue, Kansas City, Kansas, near Kansas Speedway
- Peerless Steak House, Johnson City, Tennessee, near Bristol Motor Speedway
- Sandy Point, Alton Bay, New Hampshire, near New Hampshire Motor Speedway
- Redbone Alley, Florence, South Carolina, near Darlington Raceway
- Common Grill, Chelsea, Michigan, near Michigan International Speedway
- The Ark, Riverside, Alabama, near Talladega Superspeedway

Immediately, people saw some potential trouble brewing. Would the dogs be the same?

"It goes back to the day at the Richmond track when we had the press conference about ISC purchasing Martinsville," Campbell said. "We had gone through the question-and-answer period, then I saw [NASCAR chairman] Bill France Jr. in the corner of the room with his hand raised. His question was, 'You're not going to screw up the damn hot dogs, are you?'"

France was a connoisseur of hot dogs, sometimes having his favorites shipped from famous dog restaurants in other states to his office in Daytona Beach, Florida. Despite the comments of The Boss, when infield regulars arrived at Martinsville for the next race, the world had been turned upside-down.

"The hot dogs were nothing like they were supposed to be," Campbell said. "And they were being served in Styrofoam containers [instead of the traditional Martinsville wax wrappers]. That was a no-no. One of the first calls I got that day was that there was about to be a revolution in the pits because the hot dogs had been changed. Even [NASCAR president] Mike Helton had called. It was a big deal. I had to meet with everybody and tell them it would be fixed."

And it was. There was no violence. You can still buy the Martinsville hot dog for two bucks—one of the last true bargains left in professional sports.

And you'll have company. The track typically sells about 60,000 hot dogs during a race weekend.

23 1992 Hooters 500

It isn't often that a single race ends one era, begins another era, denies a championship to a powerful veteran driver and team, and knights an independent driver chasing almost insurmountable odds. But it all happened in the 1992 Hooters 500 at Atlanta Motor Speedway. The race was the final event of the Sprint Cup season, and it was very important on several levels. In the end, that Sunday became one of the defining days in NASCAR history.

The most important event that occurred on that November 15 was a good-bye. It was the occasion of the final race in the driving career of Richard Petty, NASCAR's all-time winningest driver and—then and now—its grandest ambassador. The buildup to Petty's last race—the end of a sensational 35-year driving career and the 1,185[th] start for the seven-time champion—had been a season-long affair. Petty called it his Fan Appreciation Tour, and he was celebrated at track after track and at numerous special events as the season ran from February to November. Among the special Petty items fans collected during that unusual year were diecast Petty cars that were distributed—one model at a time—at each speedway.

Petty's winning days were long gone—he drove into victory lane for the final time in 1984—but he remained a beloved figure in the sport and a NASCAR icon. Although there was a national championship to decide that day and the race for it was tight, much of the week's attention fell on Petty. The news media corps that descended on the track for the race was boosted by hundreds beyond the normal weekly audience of reporters, and the race was a sellout despite the addition of more sets of grandstands.

Everybody wanted to see Petty's final hurrah.

No one knew it then, but in a much quieter way, the race also would start the engines of another grand career even as Petty's ended. Starting back in the field that day was an impossibly young-looking 21-year-old named Jeff Gordon. The Hooters 500 marked the first start of his Cup career, one that, like Petty's, would thrust him into the national sports spotlight and produce multiple championships and major-race victories.

As one key driver left the scene, another arrived. The changing of the guard—except they drove powerful stock cars.

Petty was the much bigger story, of course. The most important driving career in the history of the sport was ending. Gordon would go on to become a defining figure, too, but it wasn't clear on that first race Sunday how quickly his career would bear fruit. He had talent, but there was no way to predict how far he could go or how close he could come to reaching Petty's level of accomplishment.

No one expected Petty to win his final race (he hadn't won in eight seasons), but there was hope that he could ride into the sunset with a strong run, perhaps a top 10 or 15. The team put extra work into the preparation of the final No. 43 car the King would pilot.

But a fine finish was not to be.

On lap 95, Petty was involved in a multi-car crash, and contact with other cars caused significant damage to his car. As Petty regained control and rolled down the frontstretch, flames erupted from underneath the car, apparently the result of oil leaking from the engine and hitting hot exhaust pipes. Petty stopped the car and climbed out, safe and sound, as thousands in the stands relaxed, their fears that Petty could be seriously hurt in his final race suddenly gone.

"I went out in a blaze, but I forgot the glory part," Petty joked as he talked to reporters a few minutes later.

The Petty crew scrambled to repair the car so that Petty could return to the track and take the checkered flag—a finish he thought the fans deserved to see on his final day in the cockpit. That happened and Petty's part of the day was complete—a success on many levels.

At the end, after most of Richard Petty's lifetime had been spent on the NASCAR road, there were many tears—particularly from his wife, Lynda, and his daughters but also from many fans and from ESPN broadcaster Jerry Punch, who interviewed Petty after the race and could barely control his emotions.

Petty finished 35th, and Gordon rolled home 31st in his debut.

Elsewhere on the track, a remarkable run for the 1992 championship had taken place, and a most unlikely champion—Wisconsin driver Alan Kulwicki—had emerged.

Six drivers entered the race within reach of the title, but realistically, the contest had come down to Davey Allison, Bill Elliott, and Kulwicki. Allison led in points and Kulwicki (minus 30 points) and Elliott (minus 40) trailed.

Elliott won the race, but Kulwicki finished second and led the most laps, winning a five-point bonus. He won the title by 10 points over Elliott. Allison crashed during the race and was not a factor at the finish.

Kulwicki, who was operating his own team on a shoestring budget compared to many of the other top operations in the sport and who had turned down rides with other teams to do it "my way," as he often said, took home the big prize.

Kulwicki's championship run was hailed as a grand accomplishment by one of the "little" guys. His Ford Thunderbird had carried the abbreviated name "Underbird" in acknowledgement of that status.

Sadly, Kulwicki, the champion, and Allison, who lost the title on that last race day in 1992, died the next year in aviation accidents. Neither driver realized the full promise their careers held.

24 Bill France Jr.

Bill France Sr. founded NASCAR and became its iconic executive and overseer, but his son, William Clifton (or Bill Jr. as he was known) is the man most linked to stock car racing's growth and its realization of the France family's dream that the sport would become a national phenomenon.

Bill Jr. took over the NASCAR presidency from his father in 1972 and led the sport until November 2000, when Mike Helton was named president. France continued as chairman of the NASCAR board of directors until October 2003. He died in June 2007 at the age of 74, having spent virtually his entire life near the hot spots of stock car racing.

France oversaw NASCAR's first giant sponsorship—with the R.J. Reynolds Tobacco Co. and its Winston cigarette brand—and was a key player in the sanctioning body's huge growth, especially in the television sector, in the 1980s and 1990s.

France worked the NASCAR fast lanes from his days as a teenager, when he sold snow cones in the infield at race tracks and when he spent time on the road erecting signs about upcoming events. He was about two years old when his parents moved from Washington, D.C., to Daytona Beach, Florida, to start new lives and eventually organize NASCAR.

France grew up around the sport, joined the U.S. Navy after high school, and then returned to Daytona to begin full-time work in racing. He became a major player not only in international motorsports but also in the Daytona Beach community where his advice and counsel were welcome and where he made fast friends with the rich and powerful (categories that he soon joined).

Although France became a major mover and shaker in motorsports and had contacts on both coasts, he was very much at home in

Daytona Beach, where he lived in a mansion along the Halifax River. (He once said he gave his wife, Betty Jane, an unlimited budget to build the house, and she went over it.) He was on the road virtually every week, but he retained strong ties to the homefront.

One of France's favorite Daytona hangouts was Billy's Tap Room, a popular restaurant north of Daytona Beach in Ormond Beach. France dined there so often that management reserved a table for him—No. 31, over in the corner by the front window.

France often visited the restaurant with his wife, and they frequently dined with Roger and Jeanmarie Bulkley. Roger Bulkley, now deceased, was a friend of Bill France Sr. As vice president of PepsiCo, Bulkley negotiated a contract with France Sr. to make Pepsi the official drink at Daytona.

In the early 1950s, Jeanmarie Bulkley was president of the Palmetto Junior Women's Club, a group of "high society" women in the Daytona area. They had heard that France Sr. was organizing racing events on the beachfront at Daytona, and they weren't happy about what they were hearing.

Green Flag at the White House

Former president and Georgia governor Jimmy Carter is a big NASCAR fan. During his years as Georgia's chief executive, he invited NASCAR drivers and officials to the governor's mansion when the circuit raced at nearby Atlanta Motor Speedway.

When Carter ran for president in 1976, he promised the NASCAR community he would host a NASCAR party at the White House if he won. Carter followed through on that promise September 13, 1978, as NASCAR drivers, team owners, and officials enjoyed a dinner and concert on the White House South Lawn. Singer Willie Nelson provided the entertainment. Several NASCAR race cars were lined up along the White House driveway.

One of the highlights of the evening involved Billy Carter, the president's rather infamous brother, dancing to Nelson's tunes.

The president, however, missed the party. He was involved in Mideast peace negotiations at Camp David.

"People said this man who sells booze back in the mountains is coming down to start racing," Bulkley remembered. "They were very upset. They wanted to sign a petition against it. They said he was a horrible man. I asked, 'Has anybody here ever seen a race?' Everybody said no. I said, 'Well, somebody's got to go and come back to report.'" No one volunteered, so Bulkley, as president, carried her 2-month-old daughter, Colleen, to the beach-road course on a reconnaissance mission. She was sold on the concept, and the Junior Women's Club didn't protest France's activities.

The Bulkleys became friends with the Frances, and their children became playmates. Later, they shared table 31 at Billy's Tap Room many times.

"He was a very private man," Bulkley said of France Jr. "He wasn't that forthcoming, but when Betty Jane made friends and talked, he sat there and would laugh and engage in the conversation. He loved to listen to her. She enjoyed life, and he would enjoy whatever she was saying. Betty Jane brought that out in him."

In addition to Billy's, France Jr. also dined at the local Steak 'N Shake and virtually every Mexican restaurant in the area. He also was a hot dog connoisseur.

France often led local fund-raising drives. He gave $2 million to a local Catholic school and helped raise $60,000 for a foster children's program. He often made his private airplanes available to fly friends across the country for medical treatments.

Many of France Jr.'s friends remember him as the ultimate pragmatist. He operated NASCAR and his speedways using conservative business principles, and if his staff members had an idea for a new venture, he demanded that they had "run all the numbers" before he would consider it.

In the end, he had built NASCAR into one of the country's major sports and its most popular form of motorsports. Although he loved deep-sea fishing and traveling, his "retirement" from NASCAR did not include much recreational activity. Instead, he remained close to the sport and its people until his final days.

25 Darlington Raceway

Darlington Raceway, a fixture in NASCAR since 1950, has been labeled with numerous nicknames over the years. The one currently en vogue is "Too Tough to Tame," a nod to the fact that the egg-shaped, 1.366-mile track is difficult to navigate at speed and even more difficult to win on.

NASCAR's first superspeedway (a track at least one mile in length) and its first paved track, Darlington's fast speeds, narrow racing groove, and wacky design make it a venue where upsets seldom occur. It's a place where only the strong survive, where smart veteran drivers who understand the consequences of slamming the Darlington walls at high speed tend to dominate.

The races are tight, the speeds are high (particularly for a narrow track where the best race line typically is against the outside wall), and the fun is nearly non-stop.

Darlington is a pilgrimage every stock car racing fan should make. Not that it's easy to get there. The track is tucked away in a corner of southeastern South Carolina. The closest town of significance is Florence, and it's no metropolis. The nearest major city is Columbia, the state capital, which is 75 miles away.

Much of the land in the area is devoted to farming. In fact, the track was carved out of an old peanut farm by local entrepreneur Harold Brasington, who had attended the Indianapolis 500 at

Indianapolis Motor Speedway and concluded that stock car racing, then trying to organize itself in the post-World War II South, needed a large track of its own. None existed, so Brasington did what any man with vision and a bulldozer would do—he built one. People in Darlington laughed at his wild idea, but they came to believe as his track rose from the landscape outside town.

The location Brasington picked wasn't really near anything of consequence, but that didn't matter to him. He had the "build it and they will come" philosophy decades before the idea became popular.

His plans called for a high-speed big track balanced at both ends, but he had to make an on-the-fly adjustment when one of the property owners didn't want his favorite minnow pond disturbed. That explains why the track is shaped like an egg—tight on one end and sweeping on the other, and that design has befuddled some drivers for decades. It also has made the speedway one of the most famous in the world—one known even to drivers of other disciplines who haven't been anywhere close to the track.

Darlington Raceway was the site—in 1950—of the first superspeedway race in NASCAR history. Seventy-five cars started the race, making it perhaps the most confusing Oklahoma-Land-Rush green flag in the sport's history. Johnny Mantz won by driving smart enough to control his tire wear, and the Southern 500 was born. It was held on or around Labor Day for decades and became one of NASCAR's grand traditions, attracting politicians, stock car racing diehards, and fields of great drivers.

A schedule realignment eventually cost Darlington its late-summer date, and now the track runs one Sprint Cup race—on Mother's Day weekend. It remains the stuff of legend.

Darlington Raceway is the Fenway Park, the Madison Square Garden, and the Lambeau Field of stock car racing. It drips of tradition and style, and despite improvements and additions—new

Gone With the Wins

There is a long list of tracks that once hosted NASCAR's Sprint Cup Series but no longer hear the roar of racing engines.

Some of the most memorable:

- Columbia Speedway, Columbia, South Carolina—A classic Southern short track. The half-mile dirt surface served as a training ground for drivers like David Pearson, Cale Yarborough, and LeeRoy Yarbrough. The Cup series raced there from 1951 to 1971.
- Occoneechee Speedway, Hillsborough, North Carolina—A .9-mile dirt track, Occoneechee is remembered as one of NASCAR's toughest. It hosted the Cup series from 1949 to 1968, when NASCAR pulled out of the facility after persistent complaints about Sunday racing from area residents and clergy. The track's dates moved to the giant new Talladega Superspeedway in Alabama. The track area has been restored and now hosts gatherings of racing enthusiasts.
- Langhorne Speedway, Langhorne, Pennsylvania—Originally a one-mile dirt track, Langhorne later was paved. With either surface, it was one of the nation's deadliest tracks. Almost a perfect circle, the track, which existed from 1926 to 1971, produced high speeds and dangerous racing. At least six drivers were killed there. The track hosted the fourth Cup race ever held—a September 11, 1949, event won by Curtis Turner.
- Augusta International Raceway, Augusta, Georgia—Turns out that golf—as in the Masters—wasn't Augusta's only sport. The city had a 3-mile road course that hosted the Cup series in 1963.
- Arizona State Fairgrounds, Phoenix, Arizona—The track, a one-mile dirt facility, hosted the Cup series from 1951–60. It was closed after the death of a spectator in 1972.
- Riverside International Raceway, Riverside, California—A venerable road course that was demolished to make way for a shopping center, Riverside was on the Cup schedule from 1958 to 1988. For years, it hosted the first race of the season.
- McCormick Field, Asheville, North Carolina—In 1958, the Cup series raced on a quarter-mile track carved out of McCormick's baseball field. Jim Paschal was the winner.

Wrong Place, Wrong Time

One of the most beautiful speedways ever to host a NASCAR event was also the most short-lived.

Ontario (California) Motor Speedway, located about 40 miles east of Los Angeles, opened in 1970 as a state-of-the-art racing facility. It had 150,000 seats, skybox suites and a 2.5-mile racing surface patterned after the one at Indianapolis Motor Speedway. In fact, a couple of the original bricks used on the race track at Indy were put in place at the start-finish line at Ontario.

The track hosted its first Cup race in 1971 but was demolished only 10 years later.

What happened? The land became too valuable, and it was purchased for commercial and real-estate projects.

grandstands, a larger infield tunnel, improved seats, a "flip" of the track that moved the frontstretch to the old backstretch—it remains a quaint reminder of what NASCAR once was.

It should be on the schedule of every fan who wants the full NASCAR experience.

26 Lost Tracks

The Chicago Bears aren't the only entity to go off track at Soldier Field.

It's difficult to imagine in these days of purpose-built giant speedways and race tracks so fast that stock car speeds soar over 200 mph, but NASCAR has raced on more than a few surfaces one would not envision as a motorsports venue.

For example—and a big one—Soldier Field.

NASCAR's top series—then Grand National—raced at Chicago's Soldier Field (now the longtime home of the National

Football League Bears) July 21, 1956. The 200-lap race was run on an asphalt track between three-eighths and one-half mile in length. (It was listed as one-half mile, but drivers who raced there say it was shorter.) The oval track was built around the football field and inside the stadium walls on what would be the sidelines of the gridiron.

Although NASCAR's top series raced there only one time (with Fireball Roberts winning and Jim Paschal and Ralph Moody following in the top three), the stadium has a relatively long history linked to auto racing. Race cars ran there from the 1940s to the 1960s, with probably the richest period from 1947 to 1956, when the motorsports programs at the stadium were promoted by Andy Granatelli.

A Chicago native, Granatelli has a long and successful history in motorsports. He is perhaps best-known for success at the Indianapolis 500, but he also was a longtime sponsor of Richard Petty's team in NASCAR.

At Soldier Field, Granatelli scheduled weekly (and sometimes twice weekly) Late Model programs that drew tens of thousands of fans and made heroes out of the many Chicago-area racers who competed there.

Granatelli said crowds of 20,000 were typical and that one of his programs attracted more than 80,000. "When you have something good, no matter where it is, they'll go wherever you got it," Granatelli said. "Why should I do it at some rinky-dink track when I can do it in the best place in the world?"

Admission was only $1, and Granatelli was a talented showman who kept interest in the weekly racing churning.

"He was a big promoter," said "Tiger" Tom Pistone, a Chicago racer who later ventured south to compete with the NASCAR regulars. "He had guys on the payroll, 'booger artists' they called them. These guys were paid to crash you on purpose. Andy would tell them who to get, who to spin out, who to crash."

Granatelli also paid drivers bonus money to flip their cars, Pistone and others said.

NASCAR didn't return to Soldier Field after the 1956 race but now has a presence near the Windy City at Chicagoland Speedway, 40 miles southwest in Joliet.

27 Junior Johnson

In a racing career that stretched across a half-century, Junior Johnson produced results—as both a driver and a team owner—that were envied by his contemporaries. He was always at or near the top of the sport, and movers and shakers came to his doorstep for advice.

In the process of building a great career, Johnson became an American icon. Johnson is a fine example of the poor boy turned rich man—with a taste of law-breaking thrown in to add flavor to the story.

Raised on a farm in the Brushy Mountains of western North Carolina, Johnson was very involved, even as a youngster, in the Johnson family's main business—the production and delivery of illegal liquor (or moonshine, as it's often called in those parts).

As a teenager, Johnson made whiskey deliveries in fast cars, driving along the winding roads of the Appalachian foothills and dropping off cases of 'shine at designated locations in cities to the south. Then he'd turn around and head home, often at speeds that would startle passersby and aggravate law enforcement.

That experience gave Johnson a full resume in dealing with speedy cars. When it came time to go stock car racing, he was ready. He knew next to nothing about the "sport" and its ins and outs, but he knew how to drive fast.

The opportunity to race arrived in the summer of 1949 when Johnson, in an odd juxtaposition, was working the ground of the Johnson farm behind one of the slowest things in the world—a mule. He was asked to drive a race car at North Wilkesboro Speedway down the road from the Johnson place, and there was only brief hesitation. And it wasn't because he had to think about it.

Hall of Fame inductee Junior Johnson speaks to the media after arriving for the NASCAR Hall of Fame induction ceremony in Charlotte, North Carolina, on Sunday, May 23, 2010. (AP Photo/Chuck Burton)

"I had to go in the house and get some shoes," Johnson said. There was nothing unusual about plowing barefoot in those days.

Many years later, Johnson could look back on a racing career that produced 50 victories at NASCAR's highest level, six national championships as a team owner, and a spot in the inaugural class of the NASCAR Hall of Fame.

And it made him rich.

"When I got into racing, I already had the experience I needed," Johnson said. "I didn't have to learn how to drive fast. I already knew how to do it. I could run fast right off the bat."

He arrived in Sprint Cup racing in 1953 at the age of 22. During the next 14 years, he built a reputation as one of the most fearless drivers in the sport's history. He won 50 times but would have won many more if the cars he was driving had survived his manhandling. He often ran every lap as if it would be the last, and his cars often failed.

"That's the way he was," said Dale Inman, who was crew chief for Richard Petty in the 1960s when Petty Enterprises and everyone else who wanted to win races had to deal with Johnson. "He drove the car unmercifully. Curtis Turner was in that same league. Junior was hell-bent for leather the whole time he was in the race car.

"You always had to wonder if the car would hold up under him. If it didn't, you had him beat. But he was a tough competitor. The thing about him, he knew his car. He was one of the few who came along who built cars."

Retired driver Johnny Allen ran against Johnson in the 1950s and 1960s. "He had tremendous car control," Allen said. "The tracks were rough, and you raced with little, skinny tires. You had to drive it to the edge and a little bit over to do anything.

"Junior was just wide open. If it lasted, he usually won. But a lot of times the cars couldn't take the beating. It was pretty much stock stuff back then, and cars couldn't take the tracks. There were ruts and holes everywhere. But Junior was wide open or stop."

Goodbye to All That

A big piece of NASCAR history was lost in September 1996 as venerable North Wilkesboro (North Carolina) Speedway, a part of the Cup schedule since its first season in 1949, ran its final NASCAR race. North Wilkesboro's two race dates went to other tracks. The speedway, located in the Brushy Mountains of western North Carolina, had not made improvements to keep up with the expectations of the times.

Although the track's demise seemed inevitable as the sport grew by leaps and bounds in the 1990s, its departure from the schedule was received with sadness throughout the NASCAR community. A unique facility with one straightaway that was slightly uphill and the other that went slightly downhill, Wilkesboro hosted some of the best short-track racing in the sport's history.

Located near Junior Johnson's home, the track was a sort of headquarters for Johnson fans over the years. If you didn't count yourself in the Johnson camp at Wilkesboro, it usually wasn't smart to announce that fact.

Jeff Gordon won the track's final race.

Johnson's expertise in putting together winning race cars led him into team ownership, and he built one of the best organizations in NASCAR's long history, not only winning races and championships but also training dozens of mechanics in the dark arts of making cars go fast. Johnson's shop in Ingle Hollow, North Carolina, became sort of a university of racing, sending out strong mechanics to other teams through the years.

Cale Yarborough won three Sprint Cup championships (1976–78) while driving for Johnson, and Darrell Waltrip added three (1981, '82, and '85) in the next decade.

Johnson had important contacts with General Motors and used them to keep the best parts and pieces in his operation. And he pushed the rule book to the limit.

"He came to life in a hurry when he became a team owner," fellow team owner Bud Moore said. "He won all those championships. He put out a hell of a piece of equipment. He was the man to beat then—no ifs, ands, or buts about it."

Johnson was building fleets of cars when others were still trying to get by with a few cars. Johnson sold his team in 1995, saying the sport had gotten too expensive and had moved too far from the racing he had known.

"When I left the driving part, I left it," Johnson said. "When I left the owning part, I left it. And I'm glad I could do that. But I left a lot of good times and good friends behind."

He has remained around the sport, however, frequently making appearances at tracks and at other motorsports events.

28 Tall Tales from Talladega

There are wild fan gatherings on the NASCAR circuit, and then there is the infield at Talladega Superspeedway. It exists in a category all its own.

The huge infield at the 2.66-mile track has a reputation for being the rowdiest in the sport. Twice a year it becomes Party Central as fans from across the country descend on eastern Alabama to let their hair down, cheer the favorite drivers, consume copious amounts of adult beverages, and sing and dance to their favorite music. And to get involved in activities that often are R-rated (and that's being generous).

Although there is fun and frivolity across the track's infield and also in the sprawling campgrounds that surround the giant facility, Main Street for the party animals is Talladega Boulevard, a paved thoroughfare that roughly parallels the backstretch of the speedway. It is here that hundreds of celebrators gather on the track's two race

"Dang $#^&%@# Television!"

One of the most stunning upsets in Cup racing history had an unfortunate side story.

Massachusetts rookie driver Ron Bouchard rattled the sport by surging forward on the final lap and passing Darrell Waltrip and Terry Labonte to win the Talladega 500 on August 2, 1981, at Talladega Superspeedway in Alabama. It was Bouchard's first Cup victory, and it would be his last.

Bouchard's win was startling, but the real drama was occurring at the Bouchard family home in Massachusetts. A power problem near the speedway in Alabama had killed the television feed of the race across the country as the 500 reached its closing moments. It was several minutes after the checkered flag before Bouchard's family members discovered that he had won the race.

There were reports of televisions being thrown.

weekends with Friday and Saturday nights typically attracting the biggest crowds.

Visitors are liable to see anything along the boulevard over the weekend. The three Bs—beer, beads, and boobs—are plentiful. It is a tradition at several other race tracks that women will agree to expose certain portions of their anatomy in exchange for a string of beads, but Talladega Boulevard might be the national capital—at least in motorsports—of this practice. Persuasive individuals also offer free "mammograms."

There is loud music—a wild, often clashing variety of music, some pouring from expensive and elaborate sound systems erected for the occasion. People set up their own bars and serve exotic mixed drinks of every flavor.

In the middle of all this, along the center of the boulevard, fans parade by in a constant stream, enjoying the highlights—and lowlights. Activity generally peaks between 9:00 PM and midnight, and some stalwart fun-seekers can be seen partying well into the wee hours of the next day.

The next day, by the way, also holds the promise of a 500-mile race—the reason, ostensibly, that many of these same folks showed up at the speedway. By the time they pack up and head home, some won't remember anything about the actual activity on the track.

The Talladega experience is a must for every adventurous NASCAR fan who wants to take a step outside the norm. But leave the kids home with the babysitter.

29 Darrell Waltrip

Darrell Waltrip graduated from racing on his feet to racing with his right foot, and stock car racing is better for it. As a student at Davis County High School in Owensboro, Kentucky, Waltrip was a star on the track team. He set a state record for the 880-yard run. But it was running of another sort that eventually lit fires under Waltrip. He got his first go-cart at the age of 13 and soon was winning races, leading him into local dirt-track racing and then to short-track asphalt.

Waltrip would go on to a Hall of Fame career in NASCAR, winning three Sprint Cup championships and 84 races in a career that stretched from 1972 to 2000. He then transitioned perfectly into television broadcasts of NASCAR events and has expanded his fan following in that role.

It should be remembered, however, that Waltrip didn't arrive in NASCAR as a quiet, fan-friendly sort interested in learning the ropes slowly and progressing along on a course the sport's elders might have drawn for him. No, Waltrip stirred the pot almost immediately, challenging veterans, wrecking former champions,

Darrell Waltrip holds the trophy in victory lane after winning the Talladega 500 at the Alabama International Motor Speedway in Talladega, Alabama, on August 1, 1982. Waltrip was the first driver to ever win it twice. (His first Talladega 500 victory came in 1979.) At right, in partial view, is his wife, Stevie. (AP Photo/Gene Blythe)

and refusing to play the role of raw rookie. He often said what he thought no matter the consequences. He fought the establishment, and sometimes it fought back.

But no matter. The bottom line is that Waltrip succeeded wildly, accomplishing everything he dreamed of as a Kentucky kid who fell in love with racing. "Racing was entertainment," Waltrip once said. "And I think I contributed to that. I was telling the drivers that racing was supposed to be fun. You have to be able to laugh at yourself and enjoy what you're doing.

"One of my biggest assets but probably also one of my biggest faults is that I want perfection. I want my cars to be right. I want my team to look good. I want everything to go the way it's supposed to. When I see things that are so obviously wrong, I become grumpy, and I can be very demanding.

"It's because I want to be the best I can be. I am truly a team player. I'm not an individualist. I've always tried to raise the level of the people around me to make them perform the best they can."

Ultimately, Waltrip transitioned from loud-mouthed rookie to the sport's elder statesman. Fans who despised him in the beginning became dedicated followers in his glory days, particularly in the 1980s when he won three championships driving for fan favorite Junior Johnson.

Waltrip's first brush with the sport came courtesy of his grandfather. It wasn't unusual for a young Waltrip to quietly telephone Grandpa early in the morning with this message: "Don't forget to call me today and ask if I want to go to the races," he'd say. That was Waltrip's ticket to ride.

"Racing is all I ever wanted to do since I was 6 years old," he said. "It has consumed almost my every thought since those days when I would go to the two dirt tracks in Owensboro with my grandmother and grandfather, who were big race fans.

"My mom and dad wouldn't let me go to the races if my grandmother and grandfather didn't call first to invite me to go with them," he said. "So a lot of Sundays, I'd get up before anyone, slip into the living room, and call my grandparents to remind them not to forget to call me."

30 Raymond Parks

A man who spent much of his life running numerous businesses from a small office near downtown Atlanta had virtually as much to do with NASCAR's success as many more publicized individuals. His name was Raymond Parks. His story is little known among racing fans in general, but people who were involved in the sport in its building years credit Parks with being one of the pillars of early NASCAR...and in some ways, its savior.

Despite being born into poverty in northern Georgia in 1914—the oldest of 16 children—Parks lived a life of adventure and risk. As a teenager, he became involved in illegal moonshine running in the north Georgia hills and later built a significant fortune selling and delivering illegal booze and in an illegal lottery-type numbers game in Atlanta.

Playing so close to the ragged edge of the law, Parks eventually served a short sentence in federal prison on conspiracy charges but turned to legitimate businesses—buying and selling real estate, renting vending machines, and selling legal liquor—when he returned home.

Involvement in moonshine running introduced Parks to fast cars and fast drivers in the years before World War II, and his interest in the ragtag racing of the pre-NASCAR era led him to buy cars for others to drive. He tried driving a few times but quickly discovered behind the wheel wasn't an appropriate place for him.

After the war, Parks started a strong racing team that won many trophies on the backwater tracks of the Southeast, and his experience was valuable when Bill France Sr. cranked up NASCAR racing in 1948.

Parks entered most of France's races, and Parks' cars quickly became the ones to beat. Working with driver Red Byron, a World War II veteran, Parks won NASCAR's first Modified series championship in 1948. The two moved on to Strictly Stock racing, France's new series and the precursor of today's Sprint Cup racing, in 1949 and also won the first championship in that division.

As important as Parks' wins, however, was the way he got them. During a period in which many cars on NASCAR starting grids were battered and barely functional, Parks delivered his cars to the track looking polished and professional. They were numbered and lettered to the nines, had fresh tires and shiny wheels, and looked showroom spry. Drivers were waiting in line to get a chance to race in them.

Parks, with money to spend, added class to those early NASCAR races. But his contributions went above and beyond. Insiders also say he helped France, a friend, financially while the new sanctioning body was getting on its feet.

Parks left racing early in the 1950s, later saying he was spending too much money. "All I got out of it was the trophies," he said. "It was fun, but I couldn't afford to keep going like we were."

Some of those trophies were on display for many years in Parks' small Atlanta office, but Parks was a very quiet, shy individual and didn't talk much about his racing accomplishments. Eventually, journalists and historians doing research on the sport's early years sought out Parks and fleshed out his story, and he was elected to several racing halls of fame and was honored on numerous NASCAR stages.

Parks died in 2010 at the age of 96. Prior to his death, he had donated those well-worn trophies to the new NASCAR Hall of Fame in Charlotte, North Carolina.

31 The First Race

When NASCAR founder Bill France Sr. made the decision to base the future of his organization on the idea of racing American-built sedans straight off the showroom floor, no one—not even France—knew if it would work.

Would the big, hulking cars of the day stand the punishment of rut-filled dirt tracks over long-distance races? Would the drivers be safe? Would there be enough cars to put on a good show? Could the race purses be big enough to attract quality fields on a consistent basis? And, perhaps most importantly, would enough people show up to fund the purse, make money for the track operator, and stack some dollars in the NASCAR office in Daytona Beach?

The only way to find out was to take the plunge, and France did just that on June 19, 1949, at Charlotte Speedway, a three-quarter-mile dirt track now lost to the advances of time and place. It was located on the east side of Charlotte, North Carolina, and thus was within relatively easy traveling distance for many of the drivers France assumed would have an interest in his first Strictly Stock division race.

It was on this Carolina red-clay foundation that France began building his dream. He wanted to separate himself from other stock car racing promoters of the day, and a big-time event of this sort was the vehicle.

The track had been in operation for about a year but had hosted only Modified races. France worked out a deal with the owners, posted a $5,000 purse, announced the race at 150 miles, and began promoting the event across the Southeast.

Race day arrived, and as early as dawn, it was clear that France's gamble would pay off—big.

"There were fans here at 6:00 AM that day," said David Allison, son of Carl Allison, the track's owner. "They came from everywhere. Cars were parked as far as four miles away. People were trying to get in everywhere. We had people climbing trees to see. Daddy would crank up a chainsaw and go over there. He wouldn't actually cut the trees down, but they would come out of them anyway."

How many attended? Various attendance figures—from 12,000 to 23,000—have been published over the years. People who were there that day put the number closer to the smaller end of that range. But there is no question that the day was a roaring success for France and his new concept.

As for the race itself, it was barely controlled mayhem. The cars roared around the track, cutting the ruts deeper with each lap and sending a big dust cloud into the sky.

Tim Flock, a daredevil driver who would become one of NASCAR's early stars, drove in that first race. He arrived at the track without a car but talked one of the spectators into letting him race the family's Oldsmobile 88. He finished fifth.

There was nothing unusual about drivers racing their street cars. In fact, many drove them to the track, numbers already placed on the sides.

"It was so dusty that day that you would run by the grandstand, go all the way around the track and come back and run through the dust you had stirred up the lap before," Flock said. "We took masking tape, probably a hundred rolls, and taped the bumpers and

Stars Came Out Early

The first race in what would become the multi-million-dollar Sprint Cup Series attracted an impressive list of "name" drivers, some of whom would later populate various motorsports halls of fame. There were three Flock brothers—future NASCAR national champion Tim, Fonty, and Bob. All would become accomplished drivers.

There was farmer and truck driver Lee Petty, who won three national championships as he built one of auto racing's most highly regarded operations, Petty Enterprises. He crashed during the race and finished 17th.

Also racing was "Wild Man" Curtis Turner, one of the true storybook characters in stock car racing. He finished ninth.

Red Byron, a World War II veteran who would win the series' first championship, finished third. He raced with a leg brace because of wartime injuries.

Also in the field were Buck Baker, as tough a driver as NASCAR would ever produce; Jack Smith, a driver who blazed through the short tracks of the Carolinas and Georgia to make a name for himself; and Jim Paschal, a steady-as-she-goes driver who won 25 Cup races.

Richard Petty, who would become NASCAR's winningest driver, was at the race but didn't participate. He was watching his father.

the chrome, trying to keep the rocks from really beating up the cars. But when the race was over, the front end was all beat up."

Race cars had been pinged, dinged, and creamed on dirt tracks before, of course, but most of those were jalopy racers rescued from junkyards. On this day at Charlotte Speedway, fans watched virtually new sedans go through the meat grinder for 150 miles.

"We were having a ball," Flock said. "Nobody had ever run those cars before. It was real close, and you couldn't get away from anybody."

Were there safety enhancements? Very few. "One guy drove with a truck inner tube around him," Flock said. "The cars were pretty much just like they came from the dealer. No roll bars. No nothing. No one had ever run brand-new cars, and people came out just to see what in the world was going to happen."

The biggest problems of the day were broken wheels—some couldn't stand the strain of the big, powerful cars lurching through the turns—and overheating. Radiators spewed water repeatedly as cars overheated.

During the race, future series champion Lee Petty caused the first caution flag of the new form of racing by rolling his Buick Roadmaster.

Glenn Dunnaway, a driver from nearby Gastonia, rolled across the finish line first. He was three laps in front of second-place Jim Roper, a Kansas resident.

Dunnaway's historic celebration would be short-lived, however. A post-race inspection revealed that his 1947 Ford had altered rear springs. The car was a converted moonshine hauler, and the extra-strength springs had been added to support the weight of illegal liquor hauls.

It was no wonder the car was fast. It was used to outrun revenue agents.

Dunnaway was disqualified because of the illegal equipment, elevating Roper to first place and the $2,000 winner's share of the purse. He became a quite unlikely winner of the first race in what would become the nation's most popular motorsports series.

Roper drove his street 1949 Lincoln from Kansas to Charlotte for the race and then drove it home—with a new engine. NASCAR officials removed the car's original engine for inspection, but Roper was able to leave town because a local car dealership gave him a replacement.

Dunnaway took NASCAR to court over his disqualification, but the legal system supported NASCAR's ability to control the rules of its races, setting an important precedent for France and his fledgling operation.

Roper drove home a happy man. He would never win another race in the series.

Charlotte Speedway eventually fell victim to progress. It was closed when an interstate highway was built through the area. Portions of the track remain visible, however, and a historical marker identifies the site of the Sprint Cup Series' maiden voyage.

32 Bobby Allison

Bobby Allison was the prototypical tough-guy racer. Sadly for him, and for all of racing, that persona was necessary in much of the rest of his life, too.

That he survived all of life's valleys is a testimony to Allison's will to live—and his will to succeed despite the odds. That success was celebrated in 2011 when Allison was inducted as part of the second class of the NASCAR Hall of Fame, making him one of the first 10 people so honored.

Allison scored 84 Cup victories in his career and a national championship in 1983, and along the way he built a reputation as one of the hardest grinders and never-say-die drivers in the history of motorsports. It was virtually impossible to get him down.

In a 28-year driving career, Allison won virtually everything there was to win. Along the way, however, he lost so much that the sorrow could have overwhelmed a lesser man. It did knock him to his knees, but he came out the other side of a dark tunnel a strong and vibrant ambassador for the sport.

Bobby Allison won the race on July 3, 1968, at Daytona International Speedway driving a '66 Chevy. (AP Photo)

Allison and his wife, Judy, had two sons—Davey and Clifford. Both drove race cars, and Davey, more so than his younger brother, seemed to ride with the same wild gene that drove his father.

Both died, each in an accident related to racing—although not in actual competition. Clifford, 27, was killed in a wreck during practice for a Nationwide (then Grand National) Series race at Michigan International Speedway in 1992. The next year, Davey, who had raced on after his brother's death, died after being injured in a helicopter crash at Talladega Superspeedway in his home state of Alabama. Allison was attempting to land the helicopter in the Talladega infield when it crashed.

Donnie Allison, Bobby's brother, had a respectable NASCAR career, but it was cut short when he suffered head injuries in a crash at Charlotte Motor Speedway in 1981. Bobby's close friend, driver Neil Bonnett, was killed in a wreck at Daytona International Speedway in 1994.

And then there was Allison's long, agonizing struggle to recover from head, leg, and rib injuries he suffered in a near-fatal crash at Pocono Raceway in 1988. His car was T-boned in a violent crash, and only a paramedic's quick thinking—and a tracheotomy performed at the crash site—saved Allison, who was at the edge of death.

At the start of that season, Allison had enjoyed one of the biggest moments of his career as he and Davey, a rising star and an almost certain future champion, finished one-two—the father winning—in the Daytona 500. That finish is memorable for virtually everyone except Allison, who lost pieces of his memory as a result of the Pocono crash. Although he has watched videotape of the Daytona race many times, he has no personal memories of it.

It is a lost day for him, although it shines in the record books.

Allison struggled for years to pay off the medical costs associated with his accident. Doctors said he might never walk again, but Allison, as determined a man as ever strapped into a race car, persevered through years of rehabilitation and regained his speech and much of his strength. He still walks with a slight limp.

After the death of their sons, Bobby and Judy divorced, but they later remarried, deciding that their struggles could best be waged together.

"I feel like life is tough," Allison said, thinking back over the years. "Everybody has had good times and bad times. Some people have had really bad times, and some have had more bad times than other people. I feel like we put our effort in, we had some success that we're really proud of, so any time the deal comes up, I'd rather think about the successful part.

"You don't have to like what happens, but you have to accept it. I accept it and go on to whatever the next deal is.

"I know people that have lost children to disease and highway crashes, those kind of things. Same thing. It's something you really, really wish didn't happen, but you have to accept it."

Allison's long ride through motorsports began when he was nine years old. His grandfather took him to a short-track race, and he saw the cars rocket out of the fourth turn, their engines singing a sweet summer song of speed and power.

Like many nine-year-olds introduced to a new sort of experience, young Bobby was intrigued. He wanted to be one of those drivers. Unlike most of the other nine-year-olds, however, he remembered, persevered, and against tough odds made it happen at the highest possible levels.

He banged together some ragtag race cars as a teenager, finally talked his mother into signing a permission form (after running in one race using a fake name—Bob Sunderman—so his parents wouldn't know), and in 1955, off he went. He drove well in some short-track races in and around his hometown of Miami, Florida. Winning quickly became the only target. He got the fire early.

"It was feast and famine any way you looked at it in those days," Allison said. "There wasn't nearly enough money to go around. It was a 'grab it and growl' situation. With such small purses, the guy who won did all right, and all the others didn't. It made things tough."

It also made him determined.

In 1959, Bobby and Donnie, both into racing, moved from Florida to Alabama because they had heard the racing was good and the money to win was better. Bobby finished fifth in a race in Birmingham and won $145. "I thought I had died and gone to heaven," he said. Alabama became heaven, and it became head-quarters for Allison and his extended racing family.

Allison hit NASCAR's big time in 1961 and won for the first time in 1966. By the end of the '60s, he was on his way to stardom.

Even when he became a regular winner in Cup racing, Allison still wedged short-track races at backwater tracks into his schedule. As late as the 1987 season, he ran a total of 90 races. He loved the competition, and the extra cash paid for his travel as well as his toys.

Allison's early success earned him a coveted ride with the Holman-Moody team where he quickly showed how productive he could be in excellent equipment, winning 11 races in 1971. Allison feuded with team co-owner John Holman, however, and they parted ways. Allison then landed with team owner Junior Johnson in 1972.

Allison and Johnson also locked horns—this was a trend for Allison over the years, but they won 10 times. Then Allison abruptly quit, Johnson later saying if they had stayed together they could have challenged Richard Petty's career victory record of 200.

"I did drive for Junior Johnson for a year," Allison said during his Hall of Fame induction with Johnson in the audience. "Really, really should have stayed there. But I had some guy come along and tell me he really knew where a brighter moon was or a bigger pot of gold or something like that. Down the road I went. Junior, I apologize."

Along the way, Allison rooted his way to the front of race after race, relentlessly challenging the status quo and targeting the man—Petty—who ruled the sport during those years. Allison and Petty engaged in a long-running feud that stretched from the late 1960s into the early 1970s, a fierce rivalry that resulted in fistfights among their crew members and enough wrecked and battered race cars to fill significant junkyard space.

Fans even got involved. After a Petty victory at North Wilkesboro Speedway in North Carolina, a spectator who had been overserved with adult beverages lunged toward Petty, only to be stopped by the well-placed fist of Maurice Petty, Richard's brother and engine builder.

The two sides called an end to the drama in 1972, and Petty and Allison have been good friends for many years. They often recount the days of the on-track shenanigans for interested and amazed observers.

Asked about his greatest racing accomplishments, Allison divides the category. "The 1988 win at Daytona should be number one, but I still don't remember 1988," Allison said. "Some day maybe I will, and if so, maybe I'll have to change my outlook.

"But I have to go with the 1983 championship. I had worked so hard and had gone through so many different scenarios—leaving teams, getting fired from teams, all kinds of stuff—in my pursuit and finally achieved that. It stands out as the biggest achievement that I remember."

Allison had come close to the title. In 1972, he won 10 times and had 12 second-place finishes. Yet he was second to Petty in the championship standings.

33 Curtis Turner

Picking the best driver in NASCAR history is a perilous process. Richard Petty? Dale Earnhardt Sr.? David Pearson? Cale Yarborough? Jeff Gordon?

Maybe the vote of one of the most important people in NASCAR history should count heavily in this debate. "Curtis Turner was the greatest race driver I have ever seen," Bill France Sr., NASCAR's founder, said.

Turner was a racing original. He was NASCAR's original devil-may-care driver, a pedal-to-the-floor racer who lived by the win-or-nothing credo. He was brilliant on dirt racing surfaces, using a power-sliding technique through the turns that he all but patented. He wasn't the first to try it, but he was the very best doing it.

Turner won 17 Cup races over his career and scored 22 times in a single season in the now-defunct NASCAR Convertible division. He won hundreds of lower-division short-track races and was a terror on the old three-eighths and half-mile dirt tracks that hosted Saturday night showdowns across the South.

"The best driver? It was Curtis Turner," former NASCAR chief scorer Joe Epton said. "He was the best we ever had. I've seen him lose a car many, many, many times and still drive it. He man-handled a car. He was just super."

Beyond his racing exploits, Turner is remembered for off-track escapades that sometimes defy description. He was a world-class partier. He often raced—and won—on Sundays after staying up all night keeping a party alive. It was often said of Turner that he started the next party before the first one ended.

Getting Dirty One Final Time

NASCAR started its long and successful run on dirt, but it won't end there. The last Sprint Cup dirt-track race was held in Raleigh, North Carolina, on September 30, 1970.

For most of the 1960s, NASCAR had been shifting its emphasis from short tracks (particularly dirt tracks) to longer asphalt speedways, and it was only a matter of time before every bedrock dirt surface fell by the wayside.

Although dirt racing remained popular (and still does in other series today), it was not realistic for NASCAR's top series to continue running on both asphalt and dirt surfaces for numerous reasons, the biggest being that the different tracks required cars of different designs.

Appropriately, all-time race winner Richard Petty won the last official NASCAR dirt-track event.

He became friends with a wide circle of people beyond racing. He knew singer Elvis Presley, actor James Garner, and the Smothers Brothers.

A pilot who considered flying rules to be only suggestions, Turner once landed his small plane on a street in Easley, South Carolina, with intentions of popping in at a local store to replenish his beverage supply. That one cost him his pilot's license.

Turner often arrived at racetrack sites by landing his plane on the backstretch.

In 1966, having agreed to drive for Junior Johnson, Turner, who raced in whatever apparel he happened to wear to the track, was told the sponsor required him to wear a driver's suit. So he showed up for the next race in a tailor-made three-piece suit, alligator shoes, and a cowboy hat. He raced in the suit.

Turner, who raced from 1949 until 1968, was called the "Babe Ruth of stock car racing" by *Sports Illustrated* magazine. He appeared on the magazine's cover in 1968 with the title, "The King of the Wild Road."

Turner was born in the Virginia mountains, developed a successful timber business after working in a sawmill as a kid, and told several interviewers that he hauled moonshine on the state backroads as early as his ninth year.

There are so many stories about Turner that it is difficult to separate legend and lore from fact. But he was adventurous enough that it seems quite possible that many of the Turner stories are true.

One oft-repeated tale involves Turner lining up eight liquor bottles in two rows on a road and leaving a space between them that was slightly wider than his Cadillac. He drove toward the bottles, made a 180-degree turn at speed, then let the car roll back between the rows of bottles, touching none of them.

"I couldn't waste all that good liquor," he supposedly said.

While driving in NASCAR, Turner teamed with promoter Bruton Smith in the late 1950s to build Charlotte Motor Speedway. Before the track opened in 1960, they ran into numerous financial hurdles, and Turner agreed to attempt to unionize NASCAR drivers in exchange for a loan from the Teamsters Union. NASCAR president Bill France Jr. reacted angrily and banned Turner from NASCAR for life in 1961, a penalty that was lifted four years later, in 1965.

34 Carl Edwards

One of the biggest arrivals at the top levels of NASCAR racing in recent years got on track in the smallest of ways—via a business card. Before his success in Sprint Cup racing, Missouri racer Carl Edwards was one of thousands of young race car drivers scattered across the country. It was clear that he had talent. He had shown

That Backflip

Carl Edwards entered Sprint Cup racing with a signature victory celebration unlike any other in the sport's history.

Many NASCAR drivers have flipped over the years—almost all in their cars. Edwards does it without the benefit of his vehicle. After victories, Edwards climbs onto his car and performs a backflip off the car and onto the ground.

He started the practice at his home short track—Capital Speedway—and has carried it through NASCAR's Truck, Nationwide, and Sprint Cup series.

Edwards said he got interested in the idea after seeing Tyler Walker, a short-track sprint-car driver, perform backflips after winning. A gymnast friend of Edwards taught him the basics, and Edwards, one of the most athletic drivers in racing, took it from there.

The practice hasn't caught on with other drivers, most of whom celebrate their wins with frontstretch burnouts after the victory lap.

Tony Stewart quickly announced he wouldn't be doing any backflips. "Too fat," he said.

his abilities and his flair on a number of Midwestern tracks. Those who raced against him had trouble keeping up—and more trouble passing.

Yet Edwards was going nowhere fast. He was discovering the hardest thing about NASCAR racing—getting there. The Sprint Cup Series has only 43 cars in each of its starting fields. Young racers can stack up dozens of wins at their local and regional tracks and never get a chance to run a lap in Sprint Cup. It's not fair, but it's reality.

The best way to get into Cup is to have connections in the right places. A relative knows a guy who knows a guy who knows an executive on a NASCAR team. Maybe Driver A can get in to see him.

Edwards, the son of a short-track racer, got the racing bug early. He was driving a go-cart by the age of four. By 13, he had moved into mini-sprint cars. He advanced to short tracks and bigger cars and kept winning, but after several years of success in the Midwest, he hadn't gotten the break he needed to advance. He was stalled.

Then Edwards had an idea. Business cards. He figured having a card to hand to race car owners would make a more lasting impression than simply saying hello in the pits. He printed 3,000 cards—at a cost of $130—with his name, a short resume, contact information, and the phrase, "If you're looking for a driver, you're looking for me."

Edwards put a card in the hand of everyone who would take one at race tracks, and he also placed copies of the card in the classified sections of racing magazines.

"I had a lot of people make fun of me, but it worked out," Edwards said.

In 2002, Edwards landed a part-time ride with respected team owner Mike Mittler in NASCAR's third-level Truck Series. He was impressive there and soon got the attention of Cup team owner Jack Roush. In 2003, Edwards accepted a ride with Roush's team, driving south to North Carolina with virtually everything he owned in an old battered Mazda.

That began an affiliation that quickly put Edwards in the Sprint Cup win column.

Edwards moved into Cup racing full-time in 2005 and bought an airplane—he had learned to fly as a teenager—to make travel to races easier. The plane also brought Missouri and home closer, and as Edwards progressed, he realized he wanted that connection to be even closer.

"I didn't think there was any security in my job until 2005 when Office Depot signed on as the sponsor [of my Roush team]," he said. "I came down here not knowing what would happen. I didn't know if I was going to run terribly and be gone in three months. So I didn't spend a dollar. I got the cheapest apartment I could find. I rented a washer-dryer month to month. I lived in that apartment in 2003 and saved every dime."

Edwards even avoided signing up for cable television, an extreme economic approach that amused then-teammate Mark Martin, who targeted Edwards with jokes.

"Then when we got the sponsor in 2005, I said, 'Okay, I'm going to buy a house and settle in here [in North Carolina],'" Edwards said. "It was still a little hard to believe. I spent a lot of time in the back of my mind really believing all this was a total impossibility. Of all the things I wanted to do or could have imagined doing, this would have been the top one—racing in the Sprint Cup and Nationwide series, winning races, and getting paid for it.

"In 2005 I was winning races and man, I was truly just happy as hell to be a part of this. Every day I pinched myself. I couldn't believe I was doing what I was doing."

After establishing himself at Roush and proving he could understand the intricacies of race cars at the highest level, Edwards saw the need to trim his schedule from that of a seven-day racer to one that made more rational sense. He felt Missouri tugging at him, and the airplane—he now has a newer jet—made the attraction work.

"I realized I could stop at home more often," he said. "I flew home now and then, and that kind of evolved into, 'Hey, I can live where I like to live and still do my job.'"

Now Edwards, a husband and father of two, has time to ground himself and be a regular guy. "It makes me feel normal," Edwards said. "When I was in North Carolina, I felt like I was permanently away. I think a lot of people have a real single-minded focus, and racing is the most important thing. But you can push everybody sort of aside when you go that route.

"For me, if my mom wants to go for a walk or something and talk about what she's got going on, man, it's worth anything in the world for me to go do that. I go home and get recalibrated."

The difference from Edwards' early years with Roush is striking. "When I started, the testing policy allowed us to test, it seemed like, every week," he said. "I'd race on Sunday, fly back on the race plane that night, go test somewhere Monday and Tuesday or Tuesday and Wednesday, then go somewhere to talk with people about sponsorship. It was really seven days a week, which is fine, but I don't think I was as focused or as good as I could be.

"That was what I had to do then. From the beginning, Jack told me I needed to get an apartment nearby because the deal was going to be 24-7. And he was right. It's been a slow process to get to where I am now."

Crew chief Bob Osborne, the individual most closely linked to Edwards' success with the Roush team, said his driver is "still the down-to-earth guy who likes to ride his bikes and go play in the woods and hike and things like that, but he's changed a lot based on race knowledge, understanding how to race the race car, and understanding the strategies that go along with the racing. He's more a part of that than when he first started.

"He's grown as a driver professionally and on a personal level. He's still a regular guy, but he's come a long way on the professional side of it, being able to handle all the things that drivers have to deal with in this sport.

"It takes a little seasoning and understanding of the situations to be able to become the champion. We've gone through a lot as a team, and he's gone through a lot as a driver to gain that experience."

In 2011, Edwards became the No. 1 target in the driver free-agent market as he drove in the final year of his contract with the Roush team. After talks that stretched through most of the year, he decided to renew with the team that opened the NASCAR door for him.

35 The Dale Trail

Although there have been many other great drivers in NASCAR's history, none holds a place in the sport similar to that of the late Dale Earnhardt Sr.

A kid who fought his way from a struggling textile-village existence to millionaire status, Earnhardt earned legions of fans by being a country boy who made good. His story is stock car racing's ultimate rags-to-riches tale, and despite his wealth, he never seemed to lose the North Carolina good ol' boy persona so loved by his fans. In him, they saw themselves.

That legacy is celebrated in Earnhardt's hometown of Kannapolis, North Carolina, near Charlotte. One of the little town's most-visited spots is a plaza and its centerpiece—a 9' bronze statue of Earnhardt.

The statue is the highlight of what the town calls the Dale Trail, a collection of sites related to Earnhardt and racing in and around Kannapolis. The trail, one now traveled by thousands of fans every year, includes:

- Dale Earnhardt Boulevard, a Kannapolis street dedicated to Earnhardt in 1992.
- Cabarrus County Visitors Center, where maps and information are available.
- Ralph Earnhardt's gravesite. Dale Earnhardt's father was one of NASCAR's best short-track racers. He is buried in Center Grove Lutheran Cemetery.
- Earnhardt family neighborhood. Earnhardt was raised, fittingly, in an area of Kannapolis known as Car Town. It contains the Earnhardt homeplace and the shop where Ralph Earnhardt maintained his race cars.

- Dale Earnhardt Plaza. Includes the Earnhardt statue. Its pedestal has seven granite sections, one for each of Earnhardt's Cup championships. The plaza wall has 76 granite sections, one for each of Earnhardt's Cup wins. Plants and flowers in the plaza are planted in groups of three to acknowledge Earnhardt's Sprint Cup car number. Eight lights shine on the statue to honor Ralph Earnhardt's No. 8 car (a number later raced by Dale Earnhardt Jr.).

36 Fireball Roberts

It is perhaps odd that Edward Glenn Roberts, the man with the most famous nickname in stock car racing history, picked up the unusual moniker not from motorsports but on the baseball field. "Fireball" Roberts, one of the best drivers of NASCAR's first two decades and a very popular fan favorite, earned his nickname by having a blazing fastball during the days when he pitched for his high school baseball team.

The name followed him into auto racing, and it stuck. Many fans never knew him by anything else, although Roberts didn't like the nickname and urged people to call him Glenn.

Roberts raced from 1950 to 1964, when he died as the result of injuries suffered in a crash at Charlotte Motor Speedway. In a horrible irony, Roberts died because of fire. He was severely burned in the accident.

Although Roberts never won a Cup championship, he won the Daytona 500 and the Southern 500, visited victory lane 33 times, and developed a reputation as a driver who would test the limits of equipment. He was particularly impressive on the bigger speedways

Glenn "Fireball" Roberts holds his trophy after winning the first Firecracker 250 stock car race in Daytona Beach, Florida, on July 4, 1959. Roberts won with an average speed of 140.581 mph in a 1959 Pontiac and received $4,100.
(AP Photo)

that began dominating NASCAR in the 1960s. Roberts drove for renowned car builder Smokey Yunick, who called Roberts the "best driver I ever had" on more than one occasion.

Roberts' last race was the World 600 at Charlotte Motor Speedway in May 1964. The season was expected to be his last. He had plans to retire from driving and work in public relations.

During the race, Junior Johnson and Ned Jarrett crashed in Turn 2, and Roberts swerved his car to avoid them. He backed into a wall on the track backstretch, and his car flipped onto its roof. Fuel spilled inside the car and caught on fire, and Roberts, momentarily trapped inside, was burned before Jarrett, who had run to check on Roberts, could help him out of the car.

Roberts was taken to a Charlotte hospital and treated for burns. He was there more than a month before infection and pneumonia caused his death on July 2.

Max Muhleman, then a Charlotte sports writer who covered auto racing, penned a classic story that day about the driver who had become his friend. "Fireball Roberts, perhaps the most nearly perfect of all stock car drivers, is dead," Muhleman wrote, "and it's like awaking to find a mountain suddenly gone."

Roberts was smarter than the average race car driver. He attended the University of Florida with the idea of earning a mechanical engineering degree, but he quit after three years to go racing. He was intensely interested in religion, politics, and history and often discussed those topics with anyone who would listen at the track.

Doris Roberts, who was married to Fireball, talked often about what made him different. "What really attracted me to Glenn was his intelligence," she said. "His manner. He was so intelligent. I had known a lot of race car drivers through my brother, but I kept thinking this guy was special. He could talk about anything. He liked classical music, and so did I."

Roberts also was a stickler for accuracy. He wanted to help elevate NASCAR on a national level, and he paid attention to records and lists of race victories and such. In 1961, he wrote a letter to NASCAR officials urging them to check the money-won total they had listed for him.

"If you must list the prize money I've won," Roberts wrote, "please be accurate." He listed his figures, which totaled about $4,000 more than the NASCAR number.

Roberts was laid to rest in Daytona Memorial Park in Daytona Beach, Florida, where he began his racing career. The cemetery is a few miles from Daytona International Speedway, and when cars are on the track, visitors to Roberts' gravesite can hear them in the distance.

37 Are Drivers Intimidated?

Dale Earnhardt Sr., one of the most successful drivers in NASCAR history, made a mint selling T-shirts that displayed his most popular nickname: The Intimidator.

The idea was that the image of Earnhardt's solid black Chevrolet in your rearview mirror was enough to knock you off your game and essentially hand over your position to Earnhardt. He was so tough, so good, so fierce, the thinking went, that his very presence on the track was enough to convince some drivers they couldn't win.

Most drivers of the Earnhardt era considered that hogwash, of course, although the image was a grand thing for Earnhardt and his legacy. The Earnhardt estate's souvenir trailers at speedways still sell thousands of items a year emblazoned with the Intimidator lettering more than a decade after his death. The legion of Earnhardt fans remains strong.

But what about the concept? Are some drivers simply so good that their persona can carry them to victories? Is a driver like multiple champion Jimmie Johnson intimidating to those chasing him? Are some drivers so good at what they do that they virtually have the race won at the start?

The focus, said driver Kyle Busch, should be on winning the race, not on Johnson and other tough drivers and how they fit into the picture.

"They're the best of the best," Busch said of Johnson's No. 48 Hendrick Motorsports team. "They're the guys that you've got to beat every single week, every single year. There's no question that the 48 team is probably the best team in history, that they have the opportunity to win every single week.

"But it doesn't put a worry in our mind at all. We've got to be a team that can run with those guys."

Johnson's success—or for that matter, a series of victories or championships by any driver—isn't something that overwhelms other drivers, veteran Jeff Burton said.

"I'm around a lot of people that have just flipped out [about Johnson]," Burton said. "'How did he win that race? He's lucky! Pisses me off!' I'm not that way.

"I don't race Jimmie with animosity. I don't race him with jealousy. I'm envious of him, but who wouldn't be? The only way I can do it is to go out and do it."

As for Johnson, he won't claim to carry the label of intimidator. "If we are in people's heads, that's okay," he said. "We'll take it, but that's not our focus."

Their focus, evidently, is solidly planted on those championship rings.

38 On the Beach

Some of the most spectacular racing in the 60-year history of NASCAR occurred not on a giant superspeedway or on a tight dirt bullring but—of all places—on the sandy flats of the Atlantic Ocean seashore. The location was Daytona Beach, Florida, on the eastern coast of the Sunshine State. There was no purpose-built track—certainly not a course like the huge Daytona International Speedway that ultimately would be built near the city—in Daytona Beach, but there was one that was formed naturally, more or less, by the shoreline and two-lane Highway A1A, which ran parallel to the beach.

That beach-road course was where racing made its inaugural bow in Daytona Beach.

It started at the turn of the century—the 20th century, that is. The hard-packed sand of the wide beach—wide when the tide was out—provided a great place for automobile enthusiasts to test their skills. They brought fast machines from across the country and around the world to make speed runs on the beach, an activity that lasted more than three decades. In 1935, it reached a peak of sorts when Malcolm Campbell was clocked at 276 mph along the beach. The speed runs eventually moved to the Bonneville Salt Flats in Utah.

In the years that followed, a different sort of automobile activity took over along the shore as Daytona Beach officials promoted a stock car race that used not only the sandy beach but also the adjacent highway. The two stretches were connected by north and south turns and—*voila*!—suddenly there was a race track.

The races were interesting but not money-making. When the city decided to pull out of the enterprise, one of the drivers, a local

The First Female

Fans who view women racing in NASCAR as a relatively new thing should think again. The very first race in what is now the Sprint Cup Series had a female participant—Sara Christian. She finished 14th in the June 1949 race at Charlotte (North Carolina) Speedway.

Christian was so respected in NASCAR's early years that she was invited to join race winner Curtis Turner in victory lane after she finished sixth at the brutally difficult Langhorne (Pennsylvania) Speedway in a race on September 11, 1949, during Cup's first season.

Among other early female racers were Louise Smith and Ethel Mobley.

mechanic and service station owner named Bill France Sr., decided to take over the promotion. He turned the beach-road races into a success and, after a pause during World War II, returned racing to the course. With the formation of NASCAR in 1947, the 2.2-mile beach course was chosen to host the new organization's first sanctioned race—for Modified cars—in February 1948.

NASCAR's Strictly Stock division—later to become Sprint Cup—ran on the course in 1949 during its first season.

NASCAR's early warriors competed on the course until 1959 when France opened his new marvel, the Daytona International Speedway, several miles west of the shore. One of the reasons France built the track was the fact that development along the beachfront was making beach racing much more difficult to schedule.

The late Joe Littlejohn, a South Carolina–based race driver and promoter, was among the daredevils who ran stock cars on the beach. "I've seen guys come out of the South turn there late in the race with the tide coming in and slide out into the water," he said.

The cars ran south on the two-lane pavement of Highway A1A, made the south turn onto the sand of the beach, and then raced between the spectators and the ocean to the north turn, where they returned to the asphalt.

"The sand stayed wet all the time," Littlejohn said. "You were always throwing it on the windshields of the other cars. It would eventually sandblast the front end of the car. You couldn't see to drive the car home at night after the race."

It was one of the few race courses in the history of motorsports at which drivers put small mops inside their cars to reach out and clean their windshields.

Some drivers became experts at "power-sliding" their cars into the north turn, spraying beach sand as they turned their vehicles to move onto the paved part of the course. Others were not as successful. Typically, cars piled up outside both turns as they became stuck in the sand.

The incoming tide, of course, was the biggest obstacle to beach racing. Events had to be scheduled and completed before ocean water invaded the course.

There were other problems for race promoters, however. Since the course was not enclosed, it became difficult to prevent non-paying customers from enjoying the entertainment.

France took steps to change that by posting "Beware of Rattlesnakes" signs on some of the interlopers' favorite roosts. Rumor has it that his approach worked.

39 One Very Hot Night

It isn't often that races that are built up for weeks with promotions and publicity live up to the hype. The Winston All-Star race, run May 16, 1992, at Charlotte Motor Speedway, was a major exception.

The race was the first held under a multi-million-dollar lighting system installed by the speedway so that the Winston, one of the most popular races of the season (then and now), could be staged before an evening audience.

A night superspeedway race had never been attempted in NASCAR's modern era, and there was some question during the installation of the lights if the new venture would be safe. It was a gamble of sorts for the speedway, which needed a new wrinkle for the All-Star event because of rumors that the race might be moved to another track.

A night test session revealed no problems, however, and a sense of anticipation built as the race date approached. Charlotte Motor Speedway, long known for its promotional expertise, hyped the event to the hilt, using "One Hot Night" as the theme.

The race attracted a huge crowd, and the air was electric. The car numbers glowed at high speeds under the lights, and the atmosphere was quite different from a daytime race.

The setting wouldn't be enough to carry the race and make it a success, however. Hot competition was needed, and the competitors came through.

The race came down to the final lap. Dale Earnhardt Sr. held the lead at the white flag. As the field approached the third turn headed toward the checkered, Kyle Petty took a shot at passing Earnhardt for the lead. Earnhardt attempted to block but instead wound up spinning and losing the lead.

That left the decision to Petty and Davey Allison, who raced side by side out of Turn 4 with the finish line in sight. As they neared the checkered flag, their cars collided, and Allison slammed into the outside wall as he roared across the line to finish first.

The impact resulted in Allison losing consciousness momentarily, and he was taken to a nearby hospital to be examined. One

Hot Night ended with the winner of one of the biggest races in NASCAR history absent from victory lane.

Allison wasn't seriously injured and was released from the hospital the next day.

The finish and the new evening environment made the race a big hit, and it started a trend of large tracks erecting lighting systems so that their races could be moved to evening hours. Even the super-fast Daytona International Speedway made the change.

Charlotte Motor Speedway once more had led the way to dramatic change in the sport.

40 Tom Wolfe: The Last American Hero

For one very prominent writer, there was no question about Junior Johnson's status—he was the Last American Hero. It was right there in the headline of Tom Wolfe's story in *Esquire* magazine in 1965: "Junior Johnson is the Last American Hero—Yes!"

Wolfe, the lead practitioner of what then was a new form of journalism—the New Journalism, it was called—came south from New York City to write a very long piece on Johnson for *Esquire*, one of the nation's leading news, feature, and lifestyle magazines.

Wolfe's story, the result of months of interviews and research, is widely regarded as one of the best pieces of sports journalism ever produced. In October 2003, *Esquire* picked the five best stories to ever appear between the magazine's covers, and Wolfe's piece was in the group.

Wolfe and Johnson could not have been more different, although each was born in 1931 and both would earn places among the leaders of their respective crafts. Wolfe was a fancy "uptown" dresser and a graduate of Yale. Johnson was at home in the backwoods of North Carolina, either wearing overalls on the farm or driving race cars at breakneck speeds around stock car ovals.

"There are no cowards left in stock-car racing," Wolfe wrote, "but a couple of drivers tell me that one of the things that can shake you up is to look into your rearview mirror going around a curve and see Junior Johnson's car on your tail trying to 'root you out of the groove,' and then get a glimpse of Junior's dead-serious look."

One of Johnson's quotes that Wolfe remembered vividly in an interview 40 years after he wrote the story came from one of their visits to Johnson's North Carolina mountain property. Asked how much of the surrounding land belonged to him, Johnson said, "Everything that's green is mine."

Wolfe arrived in western North Carolina to do research for his story dressed to the nines in garb that folks in the mountain foothills seldom saw. He didn't exactly fit in.

Johnson cooperated with Wolfe, but he wanted the writer to get most of his information from people in and around racing and from others living in the Brushy Mountain community. Wolfe did just that, attending a race at North Wilkesboro Speedway and interviewing Johnson's friends and neighbors.

The resulting article was a gold strike for NASCAR, giving the sport prominent exposure in a major periodical even as it was trying to expand from its Southeastern roots.

41 NASCAR's All-Stars

It started as a 70-lap race with only 12 drivers and has become one of the most anticipated events of the NASCAR season. Although it has no bearing on the Sprint Cup championship race and the format is relatively zany (and fluid), the Sprint All-Star Race has been a must-see for many NASCAR fans for a quarter-century.

The race is held in May at Charlotte Motor Speedway as a prelude to the Coca-Cola 600, the season's longest event. It began in 1985 as The Winston, one of the revolutionary ideas dreamed up by the sports marketing arm of the R.J. Reynolds Tobacco Co., at that point NASCAR's primary sponsor.

Although the format, eligibility rules, and other matters—even the name—have changed over the years, the idea remains the same—put the sport's drivers in a relatively short race with a ton of money on the line in an exciting nighttime atmosphere. No seasonal points are involved, so there is no thought of "saving" a race car until the end. Hard racing is the rule.

That idea—and the fact that the Charlotte track drapes the special event with its typical pageantry approach—puts the race high on fans' wish lists.

The series of All-Star races has produced a crowd of memorable events. Fans probably could argue most of the night about the best, but here are five leaders:

1992—Davey Allison wins. Allison and Kyle Petty roared to the finish line side by side and crashed, with Allison's car slamming into the wall after he crossed the finish line first. This was the first race under the speedway's new lighting system, and it created a sensation.

1987—Dale Earnhardt wins. He battled Bill Elliott fiercely for the lead. They had contact coming out of Turn 4, and that pushed Earnhardt onto the grass separating the racing surface from pit road, but amazingly he retained control and returned to the track, still in first place. The maneuver became known as the "pass in the grass," although there actually wasn't a pass. The maneuver has taken on a life of its own over the years, and despite the video evidence, many are convinced that, indeed, Earnhardt did make a pass that day.

1989—Rusty Wallace wins. Five years into the race's history, it's win-or-nothing concept was vibrantly illustrated as Wallace, executing a perfectly timed spin-and-win move, pushed Darrell Waltrip into a spinout on the last lap, leaving the door wide open for Wallace's win. The two drivers' pit crews engaged in a brief scuffle on pit road after the checkered flag, and Waltrip voiced the opinion that he hoped Wallace choked on the first-place money. Wallace did not.

2009—Tony Stewart wins. The race was one of the wildest in the event's history. A 10-lap segment concluded the race, and Kyle Busch passed cars with wild abandon during that stretch, at one point sending contender Jeff Gordon crashing into the wall.

2001—Jeff Gordon wins. On a bizarre night, Gordon drove two cars to victory. Rain had dampened the track prior to the start of the race, and it was not completely dry when the green flag fell. The field roared into the first turn on the first lap, and cars suddenly sailed into the outside wall after sliding on the damp track. Officials decided to allow the teams whose cars had been carried into the wall by the wet conditions to go to backup cars. It was an extraordinary move but one considered okay by the race's unusual set of rules, which have been remarkably adaptable over the years. Gordon's backup car won the race.

42 Southern 500

There are few days in NASCAR's long narrative more wrapped in history than September 4, 1950.

On that Labor Day in the cotton-farming country of east central South Carolina, NASCAR ran the first 500-mile race and the first asphalt race in its history. The site was the new Darlington International Raceway (now simply Darlington Raceway), and the host was an entrepreneur named Harold Brasington.

Brasington scratched the Darlington track from farm fields near the small hamlet of Darlington, far from population centers and despite the amusement of locals who considered his project pure folly.

Brasington, who owned a heavy equipment company in Darlington, attended the Indianapolis 500 in 1948. He returned home to South Carolina impressed by the huge crowd the 500 had attracted and by the atmosphere of one of the world's biggest sports stadiums.

Southern stock car racing did not have a big track at that point, and Brasington figured he was the man to supply one. And as a happy coincidence, he owned earth-moving equipment.

Brasington worked out an agreement with Darlington farmer Sherman Ramsey, who owned the property on which the track

Renting a Racer

NASCAR's early years are full of colorful stories—some fact, some legend—about drivers arriving in a race city, renting a car to cruise around town, and returning it in less-than-pristine condition.

More than a few rental cars were damaged in impromptu motel parking lot "races." At least a couple wound up in swimming pools.

But could you get a car from a rental-car agency and run it in a race? Of course.

Frank "Rebel" Mundy did it. He wanted to participate in the first Cup race held in the state of California—in Gardena in 1951—but he couldn't find a ride. So Mundy rented a car from a local rental company and drove it in the race. He finished 11th, then returned the car.

would be built. Ramsey was among those who were skeptical of Brasington's plan, but they worked out a deal, and Brasington started rolling his bulldozers onto Ramsey's property. Ramsey made only one request—that the minnow pond he had on the property not be disturbed. That simple plea would result in the track becoming one of the most unique racing plants in the world.

After eight months of construction, the track was beginning to take shape (an oblong shape, that is, because of that pond problem). Brasington signed the Central States Racing Association, a Columbus, Ohio–based group, to run the first 500-mile race at his track.

After entries were slow to arrive, Brasington called on NASCAR founder Bill France Sr. to co-sanction the race, adding his not-insignificant stable of drivers to the show. The field suddenly ballooned in size and grew in stature.

The race date was set, and a rough schedule of qualifying was established. In part because of the need for publicity leading to the first edition of the unique event, time trials were stretched over a two-week period. The five fastest drivers each day made the field.

Curtis Turner, already building his legend as a wild man who sometimes lost a race but never lost a party, won the pole with a speed of 82.034 mph. The slowest driver in qualifying was Johnny Mantz, who ran only 73.460 mph, but he would be heard from loudly on race day.

Amazingly, the race field contained 75 cars. They started three-abreast in a cloud of dust on the new asphalt surface, and absolutely no one who participated—drivers, mechanics, officials, fans—knew what to expect. France's stock car crowd had never raced under these conditions and for this length, and many observers figured the cars couldn't last 500 miles. The drivers, too, might give up before day's end.

There was no real strategy for winning because everything—the track, the race length, the race surface—was so new. Tires quickly became problem No. 1. Most teams raced with street tires, and the track surface ate them quickly. After some drivers ran through their supply halfway through the race, team members went into the track infield and removed tires from passenger vehicles so that the next pit-stop change could be made.

"We parked the Lincoln because it burned up tires so bad we couldn't keep tires on it," said mechanic (and future NASCAR Hall of Famer) Bud Moore, who had two cars in the race. "I remember Red Vogt [a pioneer NASCAR car builder from Atlanta] had a Cadillac that Red Byron was driving, and they used 75 tires on it. About everybody ran out."

Longtime stock car racer Hershel McGriff started 44th, near mid-pack in the race. "It was incredible," McGriff said. "One thing I remember at the start is the screeching of the tires. They made so much noise. Most of us were running on the flat part of the track (near the inside), and I had a lot of tire trouble like everybody else."

McGriff pitted so often that he eventually climbed out of the car to assist crew members with changes.

Incredibly, the race lasted 6 hours and 38 minutes, a marathon of staggering length.

Among those on site for NASCAR's first major race was 17-year-old Bill France Jr., who eventually would follow his father into the NASCAR presidency. France had simpler duties that day, however. He sold snow cones for 10 cents each.

Teams and drivers stayed in Darlington for much of the qualifying-race period. Not exactly a major tourist destination, the town wasn't quite prepared for the thousands of people who poured in.

"We went down to a hotel in Darlington after the first day at the track," Bud Moore said. "We got in a room and pulled the bed covers back, and there were cockroaches big enough to eat you alive. I told Joe [driver Joe Eubanks], 'You stay here. I'm not.' We went out and slept in the car in the hotel parking lot. Later on, we pitched a tent and camped out."

The driver who emerged out front at the end of the race-day chaos was Indiana resident Johnny Mantz. He won the race with smarts, driving at speeds that protected his tires and required fewer pit stops. He managed his speed by using a stopwatch, clicking it each time he made a lap.

"Everyone had gone past me," Mantz said later, "but it wasn't long before I saw cars blowing tires, hitting the pits, and sailing into the guard rails. I kept punching my stop watch and holding a 75-mile-per-hour range."

Mantz finished nine laps in front of second-place Fireball Roberts. Two-thirds of the starting field finished the marathon, establishing the fact that the hulking stock cars of the day could endure 500 miles in tough conditions.

And Harold Brasington had proved his point. The track he built still stands today as the Fenway Park of stock car racing, a striking original.

43 Cotton Owens

Racing tradition holds that drivers can't become complete until they have what is known in the sport as the Big Wreck—a brutal, violent crash that takes them to the ragged edge and tests the limits of their bravery and fortitude.

Sometimes the Big Wreck is so big that drivers never recover their full capacity to race at their ultimate level. The dropoff can be almost imperceptible, but it's there. Other drivers notice.

One of the best examples of a driver who survived a horrific crash and rolled on to be successful afterward can be found in the remarkable career of driver/mechanic/team owner Everett "Cotton" Owens, one of NASCAR's pioneers.

Owens was known as the King of the Modifieds, winning that series championship in 1953 and 1954 before he began concentrating on what became the Sprint Cup Series. He won nine races in that division as a driver and evolved into a winning car owner in the 1960s, scoring 32 victories and winning a Cup championship (with driver David Pearson in 1966).

Owens was fortunate to reach any of those numbers. He came within inches of being killed in a gruesome accident at the Charlotte, North Carolina, fairgrounds track in 1951.

Owens had a strong car in the event, and he charged into first place along the track's backstretch early in the race. At almost the same moment that Owens was firing into the lead, driver Willie Thompson, one of Owens' friends, wrecked on the front side of the track.

"I was on the back bumper of Fireball [Roberts], about to lap him," Owens said. "Fireball went around Willie. Then people came running out on the racetrack [to help Thompson]. I could do

Cotton Owens (left), winner of the 100-mile Modified and Sportsmen stock car race over the beach road course in Daytona Beach on February 14, 1953, receives a trophy from Mal Middleworth. (AP Photo/Jim Kerlin)

Some Data Missing

The official race report from the Cup race held at Columbia (South Carolina) Speedway March 26, 1955 is incomplete. The 100-mile event on the half-mile dirt track, one of the bedrock facilities of NASCAR's early years, was won by Fonty Flock.

Average speed and other particulars? Unknown. Halfway through the race, four cars crashed into the scoring stand, destroying it and limiting the ability of scorers to record accurate results for the rest of the race.

anything with a race car and knew I had to do something quick. I turned the car sideways and was going to go around the other side of Willie, but I had forgotten about passing two cars in the corner, and one of them hit me in the left door and turned me straight through Willie's car.

"I tore his car in half and went on through it and ran head-on into the bandstand [at the side of the track]."

Owens and Thompson were seriously injured and lucky to be alive. Owens' head had slammed into his steering wheel on impact. The next time they saw each other was at a nearby hospital.

Owens was in particularly bad shape.

"My face was knocked sideways, and half of my teeth were out," Owens said. "Willie was in there in the hospital screaming at the top of his voice for them to do something for me. They took me over to another hospital, and I stayed there a couple of months."

Later that year, Owens was racing again. He said he never had trouble driving to his limits again, despite the memories of that horrible night in Charlotte.

Owens continued to drive—and win—despite the fact that the vision in his left eye was permanently clouded by the accident, and problems with double vision and depth perception eventually pushed him from the driver's seat.

He had overcome the Big Wreck, however.

44 What's In a Word?

Some terms are specific to motorsports. Within that subset is another subset—terms specific to NASCAR's version of motorsports.

Stock car racing's lingo has developed over decades, and it's often quite different from other forms of motorsports. "Loose" and "tight" are normal car-handling terms in NASCAR, for example, as opposed to "understeer" and "oversteer" in other racing.

Here's an overview of some terms you're liable to hear on a NASCAR track visit (or a NASCAR television broadcast):

> **Chute**—A speedway straightaway, or a short straight section of track between two turns.
>
> **Esses**—A series of quick left and right turns on a road course.
>
> **Front-steer**—Steer components are located ahead of the front axle (as opposed to rear-steer).
>
> **Drafting**—Two or more cars running close together that creates aerodynamic benefits to both.
>
> **Bump-drafting**—While drafting with another car, the second car bumps the first to push it through the air faster.
>
> **Tandem drafting**—Two-car drafting that has become popular at Daytona and Talladega in recent seasons.
>
> **Bite**—How tires adhere to a racing surface.

Groove—An invisible line around a speedway that drivers typically choose to make their cars run faster.

Spoiler—A metal strip placed across the rear of a car to control air flow and direction.

Bear grease—Slang term that describes patching material used to fill cracks in track surface.

Bleeder valve—Used to reduce tire air pressure.

Camber—The amount a tire is tilted in or out from vertical.

Contact patch—The portion of a race tire that makes contact with the racing surface.

Dirty air—Turbulent air currents caused by speeding cars—typically makes following cars unstable in the wind.

Dyno—Short for dynamometer, a machine that measures engine horsepower.

Front clip—The frontmost section of a race car, contains the engine and braking, steering, and suspension components.

Intermediate track—Speedway that is at least one mile in length but less than two miles.

Marbles—Rubber buildup that occurs in the upper groove on a track during a race.

Scuffs—Tires that have been used at least once.

Stickers—New tires.

45 Can I Quote You on That?

Journalists who cover NASCAR regularly are fortunate to have generally excellent access to the competitors they chase around the country most of the year.

Imagine Tom Brady overthrowing a fourth-down pass with 10 seconds left in a New England Patriots game and the victory hanging in the balance. Turn that into the NASCAR scenario, and as soon as he walked off the field Brady would have a television microphone jammed into his face and would be asked to explain.

That's basically what happens in NASCAR. After a mid-race accident, the drivers who are involved are interviewed only minutes after the crash, and among the results are true feelings, in part because the incident is so fresh.

It should be no surprise, then, that racing and racers often produce some of the best quotes in the sports world.

Here are some of the best from NASCAR circles:

"Somebody bit my little brother John's ear almost off. I think it's very unprofessional!"

—Crew chief Barry Dodson, complaining about a post-race crew fight that got a little rough

"If you're not a race car driver and not a racer, stay home. Don't come here and grumble about going too fast. Get out of the race car if you've got feathers on your legs or butt. Put a kerosene rag around your ankles so the ants won't climb up there and eat that candy ass."

—Dale Earnhardt Sr., providing some helpful instruction for drivers concerned about speeds

"He probably didn't mean to do it. After all, his wife wears the firesuit in the family. She probably told him to do it."

—Joey Logano, after a wreck involving Kevin Harvick, whose wife, DeLana, wears a firesuit similar to her husband's during races

"If there is a higher feeling than this, I don't know what it is. It's got to be in the afterlife."

—Jeff Gordon, after scoring his first Cup victory in May 1994 at Charlotte Motor Speedway

"I've got that dang monkey off my back."

—Dale Earnhardt, after finally winning the Daytona 500 in his 20th attempt

"Do you have a brother?"

—Ward Burton, responding to a reporter's question about how it felt to finish second to his brother, Jeff, in a Sprint Cup race in Las Vegas

"He wouldn't amount to a scab on Dale Earnhardt's ass."

—Bobby Hamilton Sr., describing Kevin Harvick, who replaced Earnhardt in Richard Childress Racing's lead car after Earnhardt's death

"It's better than if I had won myself. He's always been my hero."

—Davey Allison, after finishing second to his father, Bobby, in the 1988 Daytona 500

"There have been other tracks that separated the men from the boys. This is the track that will separate the brave from the weak after the boys are gone."

—Driver Jimmy Thompson, describing Daytona International Speedway in 1959, its opening year

"I couldn't hear him. He's got that little yap-yap mouth."

—Ricky Rudd, describing Kevin Harvick after an
incident between the two

"It's a stump-puller."

—Sterling Marlin, quantifying the strength of his car's
engine after a Daytona 500 victory

"It's because he grew up in the southernmost part of the house."

—Jeff Burton, explaining why his older brother, Ward,
has a distinct Virginia drawl while he doesn't

"This is my first major-track stock car win, and I plan to make it a habit."

—Richard Petty, after scoring the first of seven Daytona
500 victories in 1964

"I didn't mean to wreck him. I was just trying to rattle his cage."

—Dale Earnhardt, after wrecking Terry Labonte to win
at Bristol Motor Speedway in 1999

"I'm more upset with Greg Biffle. He is the most unprofessional little 'scaredy' cat I've ever seen in my life. He wouldn't even fight me like a man after. So, if someone texts me his address, I'll go see him Wednesday at his house and show him what he really needs. He needs a whipping, and I'm going to give it to him. He was flipping me off, giving me the finger. Totally unprofessional. Two laps down. I mean, he is a chump."

—Boris Said, after an encounter with Greg Biffle at
Watkins Glen International

"Racing was tough all the way around in the old days. I used to tell the guys in the pits that we'd race for 30 minutes and fight for an hour."

—Buck Baker

"We can't race with tears in our eyes."

> *—Team owner Robert Yates, who withdrew his car from*
> *the following week's race after the death of his driver,*
> *Davey Allison, in July 1993*

"Where's the fight?"

> *—Richard Petty, joking with reporters after arriving in*
> *the press box for the race winner's interview at the 1979*
> *Daytona 500. Brothers Bobby and Donnie Allison and*
> *Cale Yarborough engaged in a brief scuffle after Donnie*
> *and Cale crashed on the last lap of the race, handing the*
> *victory to Petty.*

46 Potholes? Racing Has 'Em, Too

Imagine racing at 200 mph over the potholes on Main Street in your town. That's the challenge Sprint Cup drivers faced for a while in the 2010 Daytona 500 at Daytona International Speedway.

The track's aging asphalt sprouted problems at the worst possible time—right in the middle of the most important race of NASCAR's season and with one of its biggest television audiences tuned in.

The race was delayed twice after a 2' x 1' hole developed in the track's lower racing groove. NASCAR red-flagged the race, bringing the cars to a halt for periods of 1 hour 40 minutes and 44 minutes as work crews dealt with the problem.

Among the results was a much-delayed finish. Jamie McMurray crossed the finish line first as winner of NASCAR's marquee race at 7:30 PM. The finish was a typically great Daytona conclusion, but thousands of fans who had started the day in the stands were gone by then, frustrated by the two delays. Thousands of television viewers probably also abandoned the race.

It certainly wasn't the first race-surface problem in NASCAR history, but it was perhaps the most embarrassing—both because of the importance of the race and the status of the Daytona track as one of NASCAR's most significant venues. NASCAR chairman Brian France blamed the surface problem on excessive moisture and colder-than-normal temperatures in the week before the race.

Track work crews tried three compounds to plug the hole during the first red-flag period, but cars passing over it when racing resumed wiped out the patch and opened the hole again, leading to the second red flag.

The race resumed for the second and final time with 32 laps remaining.

Racing over the closing miles was remarkably close and as exciting as fans could have expected, and the final two laps (on a second green-white-checkered) were sensational, with Dale Earnhardt Jr. staging a tremendous charge in an attempt to chase down McMurray.

Being Fuelish

When does a NASCAR race not run to its full length?

When there's a rainout. When a power failure knocks out lighting. Or when there's an Energy Crisis.

In 1974, problems with oil supplies led to long lines at gas stations across the United States. That put NASCAR, which obviously depends on readily available fuel, in something of a tight spot.

In what was later viewed largely as a public relations move, NASCAR decided to trim the length of its races by 10 percent that season, thus cutting fuel use. The race names didn't change, however. Richard Petty won the Daytona 500 that year, although he actually won the Daytona 450.

Track president Robin Braig apologized for the problem on what he called racing's "hallowed ground. We're the world center of racing," Braig said. "This is the Daytona 500. This is not supposed to happen. I take full responsibility. But we can come back from this. We know how to fix it."

Braig said the track was inspected prior to the race on race morning as part of the speedway's standard race-day procedures. Braig was fired in the aftermath of the surface problems, and the track was repaved for the first time since 1978. During the race, the hole was repaired with a mixture that included Bondo, a filler material frequently used by race teams on cars.

Other NASCAR tracks have dealt with similar problems. Track workers needed an hour and 17 minutes to repair a hole in the Martinsville Speedway track surface during a race in 2004. Texas Motor Speedway had major surface problems in its first few years.

The track surface at Charlotte Motor Speedway broke apart during its first race in 1960, and teams put wire in front of the car grilles to protect the radiators from asphalt chunks.

47 Red Byron

Few fans are familiar with his name, but he always will be first.

At the very top of the record-book listing of champions of what now is the Sprint Cup Series is Red Byron, a tough-as-gristle World War II survivor who won the 1949 Cup (then Strictly Stock) driver's championship, the first awarded by NASCAR.

There were only eight races that first season, and Byron won two of them—at Daytona Beach, Florida, on the beach-road course and at Martinsville Speedway in southern Virginia.

Red Byron's 1939 Ford, winner of NASCAR's first race, is seen on Glory Road near the entrance to the NASCAR Hall of Fame in Charlotte, North Carolina, on Tuesday, May 4, 2010. (AP Photo/Chuck Burton)

Including Byron, the championship team that year included three of the most remarkable men who ever roamed NASCAR infields. Atlanta businessman Raymond Parks was the team owner, and Atlanta mechanic Red Vogt built the cars.

Parks was a key player in NASCAR's early years. A man of some wealth, he brought first-class cars to the track, and his knowledge of the top drivers of the period allowed him to hire some of racing's fastest. Vogt's downtown Atlanta garage produced some of the fastest cars of the era—for racers, moonshiners, and police operations.

Byron, a Colorado native, won the first race ever sanctioned by NASCAR—a 1948 Modified race at the Daytona beach-road course. He also won the Modified championship that year, one season before NASCAR founder Bill France Sr. developed the Strictly Stock Series.

One of the great ironies about Byron is that he should not have been a race car driver at all, let alone a champion. Byron, whose name was Robert although everyone called him Red, was a flight engineer on bombing missions during World War II. His plane was shot down over the Aleutian Islands, and a range of injuries kept him hospitalized for two years.

The worst of Byron's physical problems was a ravaged left leg. Friends who knew of the severity of his injuries assumed he couldn't possibly resume the racing career he had started in the late 1930s.

But that's exactly what Byron did. His left leg was almost useless, but he was able to depress the clutch in his race car using a crude harness attached to the clutch. This is how Byron won NASCAR's first championship.

Parks later said he put Byron in his race cars on the recommendation of Vogt, who picked Byron from an array of talented drivers then roaming the city streets of Atlanta. On September 7, 1947, Byron won the infamous first-ever race at Martinsville Speedway. No one knew what to expect when track builder Clay Earles opened the half-mile (then dirt) track, and when the starting field roared into the first turn, a dust cloud some recall being "as big as Kansas" enveloped the track.

Byron won the 50-lap event at what is now the oldest short track on the Cup circuit. And, in an iconic photo shot that day, he appears to have soaked in much of the track during the event, as he is covered in the red dust of the day, a cigarette in one hand and a water canteen in the other.

Byron raced a few years in NASCAR and then moved on to sports car racing. He died of a heart attack in 1960.

48 Riverside, RIP

The runup to the start of every new Sprint Cup season consumes much of January as teams, fans, and news media anticipate the season-opening Daytona 500 in mid-to-late February. As the first race of the new year and the season's most important event, the 500 is a showcase for new cars, new paint schemes, and new driver-team combinations and is a grand display of all things NASCAR.

After almost three months of no on-track activity, it's like the dam of anticipation is ready to burst, and the Daytona 500 provides the outlet.

Opening the season in Daytona Beach seems like such a normal thing that one might think it has been in practice since the track's opening in 1959. Not true. The "tradition" of the 500 opening the new season has been in place only since 1982.

For many of the previous seasons, the NASCAR year unfolded with the Western 500 at the Riverside International Raceway road course in southern California. The Daytona 500 was the year's second race.

Although Riverside no longer exists, it was considered by many to be one of the best road courses in the motorsports world. It was a fast and dangerous track (Cup champion Joe Weatherly died there in a 1964 crash) with long straights and tight turns. Dan Gurney, Parnelli Jones, A.J. Foyt, and Mark Donohue were some of the unusual names to win NASCAR races there.

Riverside lost its prime opening spot on the Cup schedule because NASCAR's ruling France family wanted the season opener moved to Daytona to benefit from the surrounding publicity. Les Richter, the former Los Angeles Rams football star who was president at Riverside, didn't object. In part because Riverside often was hammered by weather problems in January, Richter, friends said, was pleased to move his race to November.

Riverside held its final NASCAR race in 1988. The track was sold, and a shopping mall and housing development were built on the property.

49 A Place of Honor

One of the most famous race cars in NASCAR history became one of the most visible vehicles in American history. The bright red and blue Pontiac Richard Petty drove to victory in the July 4, 1984, Firecracker 400 at Daytona International Speedway received a significant honor. The car has been displayed in the Smithsonian Institution's National Museum of American History in Washington, D.C.

Museum officials asked Petty for the car after he outran Cale Yarborough in a frantic battle to the wire at Daytona, scoring his 200th—and final—Sprint Cup victory.

Petty agreed, but not before the car was raced again—in the Cup race at Talladega Superspeedway July 29, 1984. Fortunately for historians and Smithsonian visitors, the car wasn't involved in a crash.

The car remains part of the national museum's inventory, although it is not permanently on display.

Its Smithsonian object number is 1985.0009.01.

Its NASCAR number, the one that became synonymous with Petty, is 43.

50 Smokey Yunick

The sign proclaimed the place, "The Best Damn Garage in Town." It was so much more than that.

Henry Yunick was the proprietor and resident genius. No one knew him as Henry. He was Smokey. From that group of buildings on Beach Street in Daytona Beach, Florida, Yunick sent forth some of the most innovative race cars—and racing "devices"—ever developed.

Yunick died in 2001 at the age of 77. Many racing secrets left with him.

Yunick worked with or for many drivers during his decades in racing. He was mostly associated with NASCAR manufacturers and teams, but he also was devoted to competition at the Indianapolis 500, where his adventures also were legendary.

Yunick's renowned ability to wrestle the NASCAR rulebook into submission often put him at odds with officials and particularly with the ruling France family. He and Bill France Jr. had an especially contentious relationship over the years.

Yunick took it all in stride, however. He was seldom seen without his battered Stetson, a pipe, and a stark white mechanic's uniform, and it was almost possible to see the wheels turning in his brain as he moved through garage areas.

Among the many auto racing endeavors Yunick pursued over the years were improvements in safety. Fireball Roberts, who died after being massively burned in a 1964 crash at Charlotte Motor Speedway, drove and won for Yunick, and Roberts' death spurred Yunick's movement in that area.

Among Yunick's safety innovations was the first generation of "soft" walls. He used old tires to form impact barriers to soften hard hits during accidents. His ideas in that arena didn't get very far as NASCAR officials rejected the barriers.

Yunick was an expert at building cars that fit within NASCAR's rules parameters but also had a few tricks hidden in their frames—and elsewhere. He built a 1966 Chevrolet Chevelle for driver Curtis Turner that looked legal at first glance, but closer examination revealed minor modifications to the roof, windows, and floor—enough changes to make the car about seven-eighths scale.

It was that sort of thing that kept Yunick on the defensive much of his racing career. He loved the "game" of toying with inspectors almost as much as he loved winning. He resented the fact that many of the inspectors NASCAR employed in the 1950s and 1960s were far from mechanical masterminds, yet they were serving as judge and jury over his race cars.

Yunick was named NASCAR Mechanic of the Year twice and has been elected to numerous racing halls of fame. He also owned nine United States patents.

His world-famous garage, which closed in 1987 but was a reminder of Daytona Beach's early racing heritage, burned in April 2011.

51 Richard Childress

His first race car cost Richard Childress $20.

That small investment has mushroomed into one of the country's biggest and most successful stock car racing operations and has made Childress something of a folk hero in motorsports circles. In a sport whose popularity has attracted team owners from many walks of life, Childress remains a "racer," a guy who grew up in the sport, dreamed of winning races and making money, and eventually did both beyond his wildest hopes.

It's been a long and fruitful ride for a kid who once sold peanuts in the grandstand at the Bowman Gray Stadium racetrack in Winston-Salem, North Carolina.

"I wouldn't say I didn't set high goals for myself and my race team," Childress said. "It's just that racing is such a hit-and-miss deal. I've seen a lot of people who put a lot of hard work into something and you were just sure it would work out and it didn't for some reason or another.

"I've had deals like that. I've also had deals where I thought everything should go right and nothing did. So when you get into racing, you set realistic goals. That's the cake. The rest is icing. We've had a lot of icing since those early days."

Most of the "icing" came in the person of driver Dale Earnhardt Sr., who formed virtually the perfect partnership with Childress. They won six Sprint Cup championships together (Earnhardt won another with team owner Rod Osterlund) as they built one of NASCAR's most formidable teams of the 1980s and '90s. Childress' world was turned upside-down when Earnhardt was killed in the 2001 Daytona 500 as they began the search for another title, but the team owner struggled through the pain and stayed on track.

Childress himself raced for a decade as a Cup driver, trying to make ends meet as an underfunded independent team. He raced in Cup for the first time in 1969 and ran full seasons throughout most of the 1970s before retiring as a driver—and a winless one—in 1981.

He turned over the wheel that season to Earnhardt, who ran 11 races in Childress cars.

"I had never considered being just a car owner at that point," Childress said. "Even when I finally made the decision in '81, it was the toughest decision I've ever made. Looking back, of course, it was also the smartest."

Childress and Earnhardt became fast friends, but Childress said his operation was not at a point to provide Earnhardt with race cars that matched his driving ability. Ricky Rudd replaced Earnhardt and gave Childress his first Cup win in 1983, putting the operation on solid ground.

Earnhardt returned in 1984, won twice that season and four times in 1985, then scored Childress's first Cup title in 1986.

"A lot of people wanted to see me and Dale back together," Childress said. "They thought it had been a good combination. I did, too, and I was excited about the new opportunities we had. The first time Dale drove for me, I was a little uneasy. I think anybody in my position would have been. He was the defending series champion, and here I was the car owner and calling the shots.

"When he came back, my team had won some poles and a couple of races, and I felt I had something to offer to the combination, too."

The Childress-Earnhardt success quickly multiplied and made Childress' 1971 decision to leave an automobile repair shop and go racing look golden.

Since Earnhardt's death in 2001, Childress has worked steadily to return his operation to championship caliber. When he first went racing, he paid 20 bucks for a 1947 Plymouth. The road since then has been a fast one.

52 A "Running" Finish

Carl Edwards appeared to be on his way to winning the Aaron's 499 in April 2009 at Talladega Superspeedway. Then Brad Keselowski appeared.

Keselowski made a move to pass Edwards for the lead on the frontstretch of the final lap. Edwards dropped down the track to block. Keselowski was having none of that. He stayed on the gas and hit Edwards, sending his car flying into the air and then into the catchfence separating the racing surface from the grandstand.

Carl Edwards runs to the finish line after crashing on the final lap of the Aaron's 499 at Talladega Superspeedway in Talladega, Alabama, on Sunday, April 26, 2009. (AP Photo/Glenn Smith)

As Keselowski crossed the finish line to win the race, Edwards' car wound up on the apron adjacent to the track. It was a battered heap, and a small fire had started in the engine compartment, but Edwards was not hurt.

In fact, Edwards climbed from the car, his helmet still on, and ran on foot to the finish line, thus recreating a scene from the movie *Talladega Nights: The Ballad of Ricky Bobby*, in which actor Will Ferrell, playing NASCAR driver Ricky Bobby, runs across the line after a big wreck.

Of course, Edwards' on-foot finish of his lap did not count.

One must be inside one's race car as it passes the finish line.

53 Wood Brothers

The long, eventful, and successful racing career of the Wood Brothers Racing team started with something of a downer. Glen Wood, who was making his living working in a sawmill, made his first run in a race car in 1950 at a quarter-mile dirt track called Morris (Virginia) Speedway in a 1938 Ford coupe.

"I was trying to go between two cars and hooked the left rear tire," Wood said. "It bent the rear-end housing. We were towing it home behind another car, and it was wobbling because it was bent. That broke the axle.

"When it came out, it jerked the gas spout out of the fender, and it fell down on the highway and caught fire. It burned up right there in the middle of the highway. We finally got the car unhooked from it. We didn't have fire extinguishers or anything. We had some extra gas cans and extra tires we were carrying in the race car. Once in a while, a gas can would blow up in there. We were scared to get close to it because of that. So we let it burn until it burned about everything up."

The racing team that had that rather questionable beginning became one of the best in NASCAR history, becoming one of the winningest operations in the sport's history, partnering with some of its most successful drivers, and revolutionizing the way work is done on pit road.

Glen succeeded quickly as a driver in the early years, soon discovering that he could leave the sawmill behind. "I began to see around 1954 [a year after he made his Sprint Cup debut] that I could make a living racing if I paid attention to what I was doing and didn't get careless and tear the car up," he said. "I always drove kind of conservatively because I knew who was going to have to fix it if I wrecked."

The tracks in those days, Wood said, were something less than pristine. "They'd get really rough and dusty," he said. "They had wooden fences around most every one of them. I went through a fence at a little quarter-mile dirt track. I had a little '34 Ford that I was running at that time, and somehow I got spun into the fence and went completely through it.

"I didn't get hurt, but when we came back home I got to looking, and there was a mark on the hood, a print of something that had hit and made a dent mark all the way up the hood, through the windshield, and bent the steering wheel toward me about 6". It was a board that was headed straight at me but hit the steering wheel. If it had missed the steering wheel, that would have been it.

"I didn't know that at the time, not until I got home. And I got scared then. But you put that sort of thing aside, I guess, as they do today. Everybody that races today knows it's dangerous, and I knew it was then, but I didn't really think about it. I guess if you dwell on it too much you wouldn't do it.

"Later on, when I got to Daytona and ran around the speedway in 1959, I didn't like it. I didn't start out racing to go as fast as they were down there."

The Wood Brothers team remains an important part of NASCAR racing today, having returned to the peak of the sport in February 2011 when 20-year-old driver Trevor Bayne won the Daytona 500 in the organization's familiar No. 21 Ford.

Although the Woods have been racing part-time for several years, their cars remain some of the most well-prepared and mechanically sound vehicles in motorsports. And their legacy is one of the sport's grandest.

The list of drivers who have driven the Woods' cars during their six decades in the sport reads like a wish list for someone putting together an All-Star driving team. Among them: David Pearson, Cale Yarborough, Neil Bonnett, A.J. Foyt, Dan Gurney, Speedy Thompson, Buddy Baker, Curtis Turner, Parnelli Jones, Dale Jarrett, Fred Lorenzen, and Junior Johnson.

Pearson was easily the most accomplished of the group. Using a marvelous recovery from a crash on the last lap, he took the Woods to the Daytona 500 victory lane in 1976. Pearson, who drove for the team from 1972–79, ultimately scored 43 victories with the Woods and at the peak of that period was virtually invincible on the Sprint Cup tour's superspeedways.

The team excelled with Glen Wood's leadership and the mechanical brilliance of his brother, Leonard, who was crew chief. Glen was the team's driver in the early years but decided he didn't want to stay behind the steering wheel as bigger tracks and faster speeds began dominating the scene. That opened the doors for some of the sport's best drivers.

Leonard Wood put fast cars under all of them. "Leonard was so smart," Pearson said. "He was always a race or two ahead of everybody else in figuring things out."

The Woods were one of the first teams in the sport to emphasize crew speed on pit road. They worked tirelessly to develop methods to trim seconds off pit stops, thus gaining positions for their drivers when the car was sitting still in its pit stall.

The team's prowess in that area earned the Woods an invitation from Ford Motor Co. to work the pits for driver Jimmy Clark in the 1965 Indianapolis 500. The open-wheel world was foreign to the Woods, but the team arrived in Indianapolis and figured out the best way to approach pitting Clark's car, and he won the race.

Among the drivers who raced for the Woods, in one of the most unusual pairings of the period, was Kyle Petty, son of Richard Petty. The Pettys and the Woods were big rivals in the 1960s and 1970s, so it was sort of a surprise "marriage" in 1985 when Kyle signed on with the team.

It was one of the best decisions of his career, said Kyle Petty, who raced with the Woods through the 1988 season.

"I've said it before, and I'll say it again, and I'll go to my grave saying that he [Leonard Wood] is the smartest man I've ever met who knows cars and motors and front-end settings and chassis and tires and racetracks—the total package," Petty said. "I learned more in the three or four years that I was there than I've learned everywhere else."

In 1985, Glen and Leonard passed along the team leadership responsibilities to Glen's sons, Eddie and Len, and his daughter, Kim.

54 The 50 Club

Of the thousands of drivers who have strapped into Cup cars and taken the green flag over six decades of NASCAR, only a dozen fit into a special category—a gentleman's club, if you will. Those drivers, 10 of whom are either retired or deceased, reached a certain level of accomplishment in taking checkered flags. In this club each driver has each won at least 50 Cup races.

The man at the head of the list, of course, is Richard Petty, who once won 27 races in a season (1967) and totaled 200 in a 34-year driving career. The first driver to reach 50 wins was Lee Petty, Richard's father, founder of Petty Enterprises and a driver in NASCAR's first Cup race in 1949. Lee held the win record of 54 until Richard roared past it.

The only driver to join Richard Petty in triple-digit wins is David Pearson, whose career roughly paralleled Petty's, although Pearson had only 574 starts to Petty's 1,185. Pearson won a career-high 16 races in 1968, the second of his three championship seasons.

Darrell Waltrip and Bobby Allison, bitter rivals, both retired with 84 victories (although Allison steadfastly claims he should be credited with 85 because of a disputed victory).

Cale Yarborough, one of the best "closers" in the business, recorded 83 wins, and Dale Earnhardt Sr. won 76. He died racing for the 77th in the 2001 Daytona 500.

Rusty Wallace, one of Earnhardt's key competitors during the 1980s and 1990s, won 55 times to edge past Lee Petty's mark.

Ned Jarrett and Junior Johnson both retired in 1966 with 50 wins.

The only active drivers in the 50 Club are Jeff Gordon, who'll likely end his career as the third-winningest driver of all time, and Jimmie Johnson, who scored his 50th win in 2010.

55 Gordon and Earnhardt: A Strange "Rivalry"

One of the greatest rivalries in NASCAR history is one that really never developed.

Fans, media, and promoters wanted Jeff Gordon, fresh-faced newcomer and representative of a new wave of fans, to launch himself in the 1990s into a fierce, crash-for-crash competition with Dale Earnhardt Sr., the sport's leading driver and Mr. Old School personified.

Fans of the two drivers divided into warring camps. Earnhardt fans didn't like Gordon because he was from California and didn't fit the Southeastern mold they saw as representative of NASCAR drivers. Gordon brought a new, generally younger generation of fans into NASCAR with his arrival.

It was expected that they would battle tooth-and-nail on the track, crashing into each other at least once a month and filling television broadcasts and newspaper and magazine pages with venom.

But then a funny thing happened. Earnhardt and Gordon became fast friends and business partners. They quickly built a strong respect for each other. They didn't engage in the fierce fender-banging fans might have wanted, and there were very few tense words between them.

Growing up in racing, Gordon was well-acquainted with the Earnhardt legend before Gordon's arrival in NASCAR. But he

Jeff Gordon, the NASCAR rookie driver of the year (left), poses with the 1993 NASCAR Winston Cup Champion Dale Earnhardt during a news conference in New York on Thursday, December 2, 1993. (AP Photo/Ed Bailey)

saw the "real" Earnhardt early in his career while practicing for an International Race of Champions event at Daytona International Speedway.

"I think there were probably three or four of us out there, and I know Dale was one and [Ken] Schrader was one and I was one," Gordon said. "And I was pretty new to the IROC series and learning those cars and the way they drafted and everything. So I was just kind of a kid in a candy store having a great time.

"And I remember that I think Schrader was leading, I was running second, and we came off Turn 2, and Dale gave me a pretty good push. And I got underneath Schrader and I was like, 'Cool, I'm going to go right by him.' And then before I could even look in my mirror, Dale was inside of me three wide down the back straightaway.

"It just seemed like the longest back straightaway I'd ever experienced. Like in all my laps around Daytona, it just seemed like that back straightaway went on for like five minutes, because the moment stood in time, and I was just there taking it all in.

"I just remember I looked to the right. And back in those days you had no headrest. You could pretty much see all the way inside the car. And I remember looking to the right at Schrader, and he was just looking ahead, focused, because we're three wide. And I looked to my left, and Dale is over here like—he's kicked back. He's got one hand over here, one hand on the steering wheel; he's looking at me with this big grin on his face.

"I realized at that moment I'm three wide in between Schrader and Earnhardt. And back then you couldn't go three wide into Turn 3. And I was like, 'Now, which one of us is going to lift? I'm not going to lift. I'm not going to lift.'

"As we got closer to Turn 3 and I look over at Dale, I realize I was going to have to be the bigger person in this moment and lift. And thank God I did, because I lifted and Dale went in there sliding all the way up three lanes, got in front of Schrader, and it would have been a heck of a wreck.

"I'll never forget that look on his face and just how relaxed he was in that race car at that moment when I was freaking out because we're three wide."

Earnhardt got Gordon's attention many other times during competition, but they never had a contentious relationship. Competitive, yes. Argumentative, no.

56 Carl Kiekhaefer: The First Super-Team Owner

Although Rick Hendrick was the first NASCAR team owner to make the multi-car concept super-successful in the modern era, the man who first put the idea in motion raced a half-century earlier.

Carl Kiekhaefer was the pioneer of the "team" scheme in NASCAR. Builder of the popular Mercury outboard engines for boats, Kiekhaefer, a Wisconsin native, jumped into NASCAR racing in 1955, primarily as an innovative way to advertise the boat engines. "Kiekhaefer Outboards" was splashed across the cars he entered in Grand National racing.

In some races, Kiekhaefer entered four cars and sponsored several others.

Kiekhaefer invaded the sport with new ideas and a new approach. He looked on his fleet of cars and drivers as a team, and he put his mechanics in uniforms—a first in the series. He moved his drivers from race to race in a private plane. And he ran the operation with an iron fist.

A Flock of Flocks

From its very beginnings, NASCAR has been a "family" sport. Sons and grandsons have followed fathers and grandfathers into the sport. Brothers have raced against brothers. Daughters have raced against dads.

But the concept was taken to an extreme very early in the sport's history.

In the second race of the first season of the Strictly Stock (later Sprint Cup) Series, an event held at the Daytona beach-road course in Florida, three Flock brothers—Tim, Fonty, and Bob—raced against their sister, Ethel Flock Mobley. Ethel was among several women who raced in NASCAR's early years.

In the Daytona race, she finished 11th, beating Fonty (19th) and Bob (22nd). Tim Flock finished second to winner Red Byron, who was also the champion of NASCAR's first Cup season.

The late Tim Flock, who raced for Kiekaefer and won the national title in 1955, remembered him as a demanding and unusual owner who asked much of his drivers.

"He would rent motels for the drivers and the teams, and he wouldn't allow the drivers to sleep with their wives the night before a race," Flock said. "He was a strange, strange guy."

Kiekhaefer left NASCAR in 1956, apparently dissatisfied with the promotional value of the sport and disgruntled after disputes with NASCAR. He died in 1983.

57 Race Day—A Long Day

When the green flag drops (typically in the early afternoon on Sundays) to officially start a Sprint Cup race, most of the drivers in the field already have put in a full day outside the race car.

Race Day is work day for NASCAR drivers—and that encompasses much more than being wheelmen. The day typically begins in early- to mid-morning (depending on the race start time) with the driver making what's called a "hospitality" appearance somewhere on the speedway grounds. This usually happens in a speedway suite or an infield tent or another enclosure at the track site where representatives of one or more of the driver's sponsors have gathered. The driver typically will give a short talk and answer questions and perhaps sign a few autographs.

Some drivers also spend part of race morning at one of their souvenir trailers, signing autographs for fans who picked up tickets to get spots in the autograph line.

Next on the list is the drivers' meeting, held two hours before the start of the race. Here drivers, crew chiefs, and other important team members view a video providing instructions about the day's race, and special guests are introduced to the crowd.

Generally, a short church service is held after the drivers' meeting, and many team members stay for that service.

In the hour before the race start, drivers in the starting field are introduced to the crowd in a session that is wildly elaborate at some tracks. Often, the competitors are driven around the track in the back of a pickup truck or in a convertible so that fans in grandstands can see them.

After the race, most of the drivers head home immediately—often on private jets. The drivers who finish first, second, and third are required to visit the track's infield media center for press conferences with the assembled media.

The driver who wins the race also poses for hundreds of photographs and does interviews in victory lane, a session that typically lasts more than an hour.

It's a long day—and a longer one for the winner.

The winner, though, usually doesn't complain.

58 Staying on Course— NASCAR's Course, of Course

Only 43 drivers participate in each Sprint Cup race. Clearly, it's a select group.

There are thousands of drivers competing at a wide variety of regional tracks across the United States—and elsewhere—virtually every week, many of them longing to be at the sport's top level. A tiny percentage actually arrives on the Sprint Cup plateau, and many of those are there only for a cup of coffee before finding their dreams dashed.

When NASCAR's Bill France Sr. put his organization on the map in 1948, he made a decision that turned out to be one of his most important. He wanted NASCAR drivers to be just that— NASCAR drivers. He wanted them to pursue NASCAR race wins and NASCAR championships—and nothing else. There were other racing organizations staging events and championship series in those years, but France would tolerate no straying by "his boys."

He realized the importance of developing a core group of solid and dependable teams and racers who could be counted on to be at virtually every venue NASCAR visited. So France made it clear that any NASCAR driver who wandered off—even occasionally—to participate in another series would be penalized, thus limiting his chances to do well in NASCAR circles.

One of the first drivers—perhaps *the* first—to feel the impact of France's demand was Red Byron, the first champion of what would become the Sprint Cup Series. Byron won the championship in 1949, the first year of Strictly Stock (later Grand National and much later Sprint Cup) racing.

Byron also ran well early in the 1950 NASCAR season, but he also participated in some races sanctioned by other organizations, and France stepped in. France immediately stripped Byron of the points he had earned in the NASCAR races. It didn't seem particularly fair, but that didn't matter to France. It was his way or the highway.

In the mid-1970s, NASCAR developed a number of contingency programs that paid teams "up-front" money per race if they agreed to enter their cars in every Cup race during the season. This allowed promoters to advertise that every star would be on hand when the circuit arrived at his track, a concept that served the speedways—and NASCAR—well.

The idea of "perfect attendance" now is so ingrained in the sport that the thought of a series regular missing a race—other than because of a very serious injury—is almost comical.

But France's original plan to limit NASCAR regulars to compete only in the NASCAR series dissolved many years ago. Now, despite a busy schedule that includes 36 Cup races from February to November, and despite finally reaching the top of the racing pyramid, many Cup drivers choose to race in other kinds of cars, for other sanctioning bodies, and even in relatively insignificant 50-lap features at dirt tracks far from the beaten path.

NASCAR has no control over this sort of activity and, in fact, generally supports it because the additional exposure is good for the sport. Now the pushback against drivers "wandering" generally comes from team owners. Some don't want their drivers risking injury in other forms of racing, and some driver contracts include sections forbidding them from participation in certain activities, including risky pastimes like motorcycle racing and parachuting.

Over the years, some NASCAR drivers have raced at almost every workable opportunity. Drivers like Bobby Allison, Ken Schrader, Kyle Busch, and Tony Stewart might show up at a dirt-track feature somewhere in the badlands just for the fun of it.

Stewart, now a team owner-driver, hasn't wavered from his thinking that drivers should pursue their craft wherever it takes them. The risk of injury—or worse—shouldn't be a deterrent, he said. He raced a lot on the side while driving for Joe Gibbs Racing in the years before he became a partner in Stewart-Haas Racing.

"I don't care what anybody else thinks about it," Stewart said. "I'm going to live my life the way I want. I encourage Ryan [Newman, his teammate at Stewart-Haas Racing] to do the same thing. We make sure the car is as safe as it can be. We make sure we have just as good of seats in our cars. We have the same seat belts, wear the same helmets.

"We can get hurt driving down the street just as easy, if not easier, than driving a racecar. The people that say that don't drive racecars and don't know what it's like. To me, you only get one chance at life. You need to live it the way you want to live it. Not worrying about what can happen—worry about what you're making happen."

59 Bodine's Bobsleds

There is no logical connection between stock car racing and bob-sledding. The two sports would seem as far apart as French cuisine and speedway hotdogs. Yet Geoffrey Bodine created a connection, and it played no small part in the success of the United States Olympic bobsled team at the 2010 Winter Olympics.

The story began for Bodine, a veteran NASCAR racer, in 1992. He watched the Winter Olympics on television and developed an avid interest in the bobsledding competition. He grew more disappointed by the minute as American bobsledders failed to produce serious threats to the medal winners. When Bodine discovered that the U.S. competitors were racing in sleds built outside the United States, his dismay was multiplied. "We were losing," he said, "and we didn't even have our own sleds."

Bodine, who knows a thing or two about making vehicles go fast (although on a decidedly different landscape), decided to "adopt" the U.S. bobsledding program. He talked to the people in charge, began raising money, and ignited a project to assist the U.S. program in building its own sleds and in making them as competitive as time, money, and American expertise would allow. He knew it would be a long journey, but he was determined.

Bodine wanted to see gold medals hanging from the Americans' necks, and he set that goal as one that would not be denied. He sought out and signed up aerodynamic experts and anyone else who might be able to generate significant progress in the U.S. program. And he raised funds to make it all happen.

Improvement was slow but steady. In 1998, the U.S. team barely missed winning a medal. In 2002, the team won silver and bronze.

Approaching the 2010 games in Vancouver, Canada, there was hope that the U.S. men could win the gold for the first time since the 1948 Olympics in Switzerland. It had been a long, frustrating drought.

Now a part-time racer, Bodine was in Vancouver to see the dream fulfilled as the Steve Holcomb-piloted "Night Train" sled outran the rest of the world, carrying Americans to bobsled gold for the first time in 62 years.

There followed a celebration unlike any in recent U.S. Olympic history. And Bodine was in the middle of it.

"I'm humbled by it," Bodine said. "I'm in awe of what happened. It is so cool to hang out with people from all around the world. You can't understand them most of the time, but it was incredible to be in that environment."

The gold-medal win came down to the final run by the U.S., and Holcomb and his crew completed it with apparent ease, even on the world's fastest—and one of its most dangerous—tracks.

"I was pretty calm watching the last run," said Bodine, who was among the first to reach the team to offer congratulations. "I went down to the finish area and hoped they were going to pull it off. I've raced a few years in my life, and I understand that getting nervous doesn't help. Whatever happens, happens.

"In reality, I'm very satisfied just giving our athletes American-made bobsleds. I'm just happy we're there and that they have those sleds to use."

There were obstacles along the way as Bo-Dyn Bobsled Project designers sought to build the best possible sled. "There were many, but I'm a hard-headed Yankee," Bodine said. "It was very difficult. We probably should have quit the third day. That's how tough it's been. But I can afford to put my money where my mouth is, and we kept the program going."

As part of the fund-raising arm of the project, Bodine invited fellow NASCAR drivers to the bobsled track in Lake Placid, New York, every winter to make exhibition runs and to get a firsthand look at the process.

It was part of the long trip that led to gold.

After the win, members of the U.S. team accompanied Bodine to NASCAR events to share the joy—and to allow many NASCAR drivers and team members to hold the gold medals.

60 A Rare Black Day for Rudd

Playing loose with the rulebook—both in car preparation and on-track competition—has been part of NASCAR racing from its very beginnings.

It isn't overly unusual for cars that do well in a race—even the winner's car—to be found lacking in NASCAR's post-race inspection. The front end might be too low. The rear end might be too high. The engine might be a tad too big. Fines and penalties—some severe—typically follow.

But NASCAR almost always avoids the ultimate penalty—taking a win away from a driver after he or she has taken the checkered flag. NASCAR continues to live by the thought originally expressed by organization founder Bill France Sr.—that fans who saw a particular driver win a race should be able to leave the track after the event knowing that the result would stand.

Occasionally, however, the strong arm of the NASCAR law steps in and takes tough action against winners.

In 1991, Ricky Rudd finished first in the Banquet Frozen Foods 300 at Infineon Raceway in Sonoma, California. On his way to the win (and on the next-to-last lap), Rudd shoved Davey Allison out of first place and inherited the spot.

NASCAR black-flagged Rudd as he passed the start-finish line and then waved the checkered flag over Allison, giving him the win although he finished behind Rudd. Later, NASCAR announced that it had penalized Rudd five seconds, thus putting him one second behind Allison in the finish order.

61 The Best Trivia Question

Like most other professional sports, NASCAR is speckled with statistics, records, and numbers in all sorts of categories. A jumbled mass of figures leads to trivia of all sorts, and NASCAR has its share of wildly unusual information that will be of real value only if you happen to be on *Jeopardy* when the motorsports category pops up.

What's the best all-time NASCAR trivia question?

That's up for debate, of course, but it's easy to argue for this one: Which driver finished second in the 1984 Firecracker 400, the race in which the sport's all-time victory king, Richard Petty, won for the 200th—and last—time?

The most obvious answer, which is often incorrect when one is playing these games—is Cale Yarborough. After all, Petty and Yarborough engaged in a tense and entertaining battle to the finish line with the victory in the balance, their cars banging together as they approached the line with thousands of fans on their feet and President Ronald Reagan watching at the track.

Petty nudged past Yarborough, one of his biggest rivals, and he finally reached the 200 mark, a number none of his contemporaries even approached and one that will stand the test of time as NASCAR's best.

Yarborough, however, did not finish second.

The race finish was set up by a caution flag when Doug Heveron's car spun with three laps remaining. Petty and Yarborough were running a close one-two at that point. It became clear almost immediately that the driver leading the next lap—the race back to the caution flag—would win the race because there were not enough laps remaining to restart the event under green. (Current rules have virtually eliminated that sort of finish.)

Petty and Yarborough gunned their cars down the backstretch, and Yarborough moved alongside Petty. They raced side by side through Turn 4 and to the finish line, their fenders rattling as Petty won by a few feet as they completed the 158th of 160 scheduled laps.

Yarborough, who later said he had misread the flagman's hand signal indicating the number of laps remaining, drove his car onto pit road as the field completed the 159th lap, assuming the race was over. But with another lap to complete under caution, the field motored around the track one final time, and Yarborough's move off the track gave second place to the man who is the answer to the trivia question—Harry Gant.

62 Daytona International Speedway

The NASCAR Sprint Cup Series races from East to West and from North to South, at tracks big and small, old and new. The circuit stops at such venerable facilities as Indianapolis Motor Speedway, Darlington Raceway, and Martinsville Speedway.

But *the* race in NASCAR is the Daytona 500, and *the* track is Daytona International Speedway. The Daytona 500 was not the first NASCAR 500-miler (the Southern 500 at Darlington owns that distinction), and Darlington also recorded almost a decade's worth of superspeedway races before Daytona opened and hosted its first in 1959.

But Daytona, NASCAR founder Bill France Sr.'s baby and a track that was far ahead of its time, quickly became the place to race upon its 1959 debut. The track is huge—a 2.5-mile trioval, and its infield is massive, big enough to include Lake Lloyd, a water enclosure of no small size. When the first generation of Daytona racers rolled through the twin tunnels under Turn 4 and got their first look at the place, they were stunned.

And they hadn't even gotten on the track. Accustomed to speedways of much smaller size, they were amazed at the huge infield and the fact that they could barely see to the other end of the track.

When drivers hit the track for opening laps, their cars behaved strangely in the high winds and on the high banks. It was the dawn of a new era for NASCAR—one that would produce ever-faster speeds, bigger tracks, and increasing danger.

It wasn't that the track was tough to drive. It was wide and fast, and Fireball Roberts famously said "even a gorilla" could drive a race car on it.

Daytona was a marvel, and it was different. Word spread quickly as drivers made their first laps on the fresh track, and there was wonder across the stock car racing community about this new place. Soon, Daytona became the place every Saturday-night short-track racer around the country longed to see and drive on.

It certainly didn't hurt that the first race—held February 22, 1959—had a classic finish, one that would be talked about and argued over for decades to come.

Remarkably, the first long-distance race scheduled at the track was completed with no caution flags despite its newness. A crowd of more than 40,000 turned out to see Bill France's still-young racing division run 500 miles at speeds—Bob Welborn was the top qualifier at 140.121 mph—that most of the drivers could only have imagined when they stepped onto the track grounds.

After almost four hours of racing, the chase for the checkered flag was between two drivers—Lee Petty and Johnny Beauchamp.

As they raced to the finish line, the lapped car of Joe Weatherly popped into the picture—literally. The three cars crossed the line side-by-side-by-side, and it was difficult to determine a winner between Petty and Beauchamp.

France, watching the race from low in the frontstretch grand-stand, thought Beauchamp had edged Petty. Others were certain Petty had barely won.

Beauchamp was declared the winner and enjoyed the fruits of the 500's first victory lane. But the decision was wrapped in doubt, and France and other NASCAR officials began a review of the finish.

The fact that officials weren't sure about the winner might have been embarrassing. Instead, it became a big moment for France and a sport still trying to find its footing.

After several days of studying photos—including photographer T. Taylor Warren's classic shot of the cars crossing the line—and film, France reversed his decision and declared Petty the winner.

It was a controversial weekend, but that brought a lot of pub-licity to the race and to France's new behemoth of a track. The Daytona 500 was the talk of the sports world. That set the template for what would become known as the Great American Race. The 500 gained in popularity every year, and it quickly became the sport's biggest event—and offered its biggest payday. It became the race every driver wanted to win.

The speedway was a sensation from the beginning. More than fifty years later, it's the cathedral of stock car racing. It's the track where the chill of adventure that permeates NASCAR comes through most vividly—a special place in the motorsports world.

63 Rick Hendrick

"Team" racing was frowned upon for much of NASCAR history.

Prior to the mid-1980s, many drivers saw having a teammate as a negative. They didn't want the attention of the owner and the technical staff divided. Every team could have only one "A" driver, the thinking went, and teams having two or more cars would dilute strength and take away from the mission of each part of the unit.

Then along came Rick Hendrick, a successful car dealer and drag boat racer who jumped into the sport on a wing and a prayer in 1984. He started with one driver—Geoff Bodine—and needed some timely sponsorship assistance to keep the team afloat, but he saw strength in the idea of a huge, multi-car operation and set about making it happen.

By 1986, Hendrick was running full schedules with Bodine and Tim Richmond, and they combined for nine wins that season, rapidly proving that more than one driver based in the same headquarters could succeed. Hendrick expanded to three teams and then to four, and now his trophy and championship collections have mushroomed to spectacular proportions.

More than 500 employees work on the Hendrick "campus" near Charlotte Motor Speedway in North Carolina, and Hendrick Motorsports is recognized as one of the leading motorsports operations in the world. It started with only five employees and a 5,000-sq. ft. rented garage.

The Hendrick multi-team template became one that many others have adopted, and now single-car operations find themselves struggling to keep up with the technologies and personnel numbers of the "super" teams.

Dale Earnhardt Jr. (right) talks with team owner Rick Hendrick (left) before qualifying for the Coca-Cola 600 in Concord, North Carolina, on Thursday, May 26, 2011. (AP Photo/Chuck Burton)

"The key to this business and any business is having good people," Hendrick said. "I've been blessed with some really good folks who've stayed here. We've done this over a period of years. But I never thought it would get as big as it is, and sometimes it's a little scary."

But it has worked—and worked on an unprecedented level.

"When I joined this team, everybody said, 'Boy, you're making a big mistake. They have a multi-car team, and that's never going to work,'" said Terry Labonte, who drove for Hendrick from 1994–2006, winning the Cup championship in 1996. "Now, you have to have a multi-car team."

The Hendrick success builds on itself. It's a giant that led Jimmie Johnson to a record-breaking run of five straight Sprint Cup championships.

"When you look back to where we came from and where we are today, we've got a big gorilla," Hendrick said. "We can't stop. We have to feed the monster.

"Now it almost becomes like the pressure of taking care of the people. We give them anniversary watches and all that, but they put their hearts and souls into this, and that's the pressure of 550 people depending on us so that they don't have to look for another job next week or next year. That's a lot of pressure."

There were "team" operations in the early years of NASCAR—Carl Kiekhaefer's short but successful run through the sport in the 1950s is a prime example—but Hendrick made the concept work in the modern era.

And it keeps working.

64 Kyle's Ride

It started as a rather innocent discussion between Kyle Petty and several friends about a cross-country motorcycle ride. It has become one of the off-track highlights of the NASCAR year.

The Kyle Petty Charity Ride Across America, typically held in late spring, is a fundraiser for the Victory Junction Gang Camp, the children's camp the Petty family built to honor the memory of their late son, Adam. The camp, which opened in 2004, serves chronically ill children who otherwise would miss the summer-camp experience.

For 17 years, Petty and dozens of other motorcycle riders have joined for a once-a-year ride along a selected route, one that differs each time. The 2011 ride began in Lake Placid, New York, and ended in Amelia Island, Florida. Other rides have taken the group from the West Coast to a finish in North Carolina.

Along the way, Petty and other riders, including current and former NASCAR stars and other sports personalities, meet and greet fans, sign autographs, and accept donations—from big checks written by companies to pocket change offered by children along the route—for the camp. The ride also has benefited other charities over the years.

Although the ride has evolved into a monster production since its humble beginnings as a fun run for Petty and a few friends, Petty keeps the week rolling along in his role as chief media spokesman and trail boss. It is one of his great passions.

"He rides sometimes out front of the group because he has a media appearance ahead or another obligation," said Diane Hough, the president and executive director of Kyle Petty Charity Ride and the event's organizer since the beginning. "But, other than that, he's back and forth, in and out of the group [of riders]. He's very hands-on, very accessible."

The ride has raised more than $14 million for the camp and other children's charities. Often along the ride route, on the secondary-road sections, children or families will be waiting along the road holding signs urging Petty to stop to pick up a donation.

"They'll be holding a sign with something like 'Please Stop For My Change,'" Hough said. "Kyle always stops to greet and thank them. People come out just to see him. It's all very up-close and personal."

The complex nature of the ride—participants travel through numerous states and obviously require food, lodging, and fuel—demands year-round work and planning. It typically runs like

Kyle Petty (center) signs autographs at a gas station during a stop in the Kyle Petty Charity Ride Across America in Francis Creek, Wisconsin, on Sunday, July 13, 2008. The ride benefits Victory Junction Gang Camp and other children's charities. More than 250 motorcycle enthusiasts participated in the ride that year and traveled more than 2,300 miles from Michigan to Georgia.
(AP Photo/Herald Times Reporter, Sue Pischke)

clockwork, and many of the riders return year after year to renew friendships made on past rides and see parts of the country they haven't visited on two wheels. And, of course, to help the Pettys with a great cause.

"We have a lot of logistics to handle and things to take care of to make it all work," Hough said. "It's all very organized, but the heart is still there. It still has that incredible feeling that it's always had. It's an opportunity for fellowship and being together and people doing what they love to do while also helping out."

Petty opens every day of the ride with information about the road ahead and offers a prayer. There are "pit stops" for meals and fuel, and fans typically gather at those locations.

"Kyle is very upbeat and very relaxed," Hough said. "He's very comfortable in every cap he wears on the ride. He's very grateful for the support of the participants, and he makes sure everybody on the ride knows that. And he'll sign and interact with the fans at every stop."

65 The Race That Wasn't

When Bill France Sr., NASCAR's founder, built Daytona International Speedway in Daytona Beach, Florida, in the late 1950s, many racing observers viewed the giant track, unlike any other race course in the country, as France's ultimate achievement.

Speeds at Daytona stunned drivers and fans, and the size of the track—2.5 miles with high banks on each end—was unlike anything the sport had seen.

Few expected any other place to challenge Daytona's unique qualities. But France, always a big thinker, had other ideas.

A few years after the Daytona track opened with a sensational inaugural Daytona 500, France went looking for bigger things. He wanted to build a track a little bigger and a little faster than Daytona, and he wanted to take advantage of the growth pattern that NASCAR had established in the 1960s.

With the aid of several of his lieutenants, France began looking for property in the Southeast for his newest speed plant. He targeted land near the South Carolina town of Spartanburg, long a racing hotbed. But residents near the proposed track site mounted stiff opposition, and France, who typically didn't back down from fights but didn't enjoy long extended ones, moved on.

His next choice was property in eastern Alabama between Birmingham and Atlanta. The location was the site of an abandoned airport, and it seemed ideal. The deal was struck, and construction began on what would become Alabama International Motor Speedway (now Talladega Superspeedway).

The track was 2.66 miles in length—NASCAR's longest—and its soaring turn banking guaranteed remarkably high speeds. Too high, in fact.

The track's layout produced speeds that crossed the 200-mph barrier. At that point in history, that was too fast (and still is, many claim). And therein rested the problem that cast a big cloud over the debut of France's monster accomplishment.

There were early signs of trouble as teams prepared for the first race—the Talladega 500 of September 14, 1969. The first laps were shocking; Charlie Glotzbach ran 199.987 mph in practice, and then he planted his car on the pole at 199.466.

More troubling than the high speeds was the fact that the tires Goodyear and Firestone had manufactured for the track were no match for the conditions. They came apart after only a few laps,

Numbers You Won't See Again

It is said that every record is made to be broken. In NASCAR, however, one is likely to stand the test of time.

On April 30, 1987, at Talladega Superspeedway in Alabama, Bill Elliott set a record qualifying speed—212.809 mph—that probably will stand forever. After Elliott's blistering run, the 500 was marred by a violent crash by Bobby Allison, whose car flipped on the frontstretch and almost sailed into the grandstand. That convinced NASCAR officials to slow Cup cars with the use of restrictor plates, devices that slow the flow of air and fuel into intake manifolds and thus limit speeds.

The plates have been in use at Talladega Superspeedway and Daytona International Speedway since that time, and as speeds have risen to the 200-mph mark at other tracks, other speed-sapping rule changes have been made.

It is very unlikely that any future NASCAR event will see the sort of speed Elliott recorded on that day at Talladega.

clearly creating dangerous conditions, especially on such a fast track.

Instead of a celebration and the unveiling of a great new speed-plant, the opening week at Talladega became a circus. Drivers and teams immediately voiced their concerns about the tire situation. France didn't deny the problem, but his advice rattled the driver corps—simply race at speeds that are safe for the tires, France said. That idea went over like cheap umbrellas on a rainy day.

The tire companies worked with different tire compounds, but nothing was a match for the track, which drivers described as rough and not ready to be raced on. "It's the roughest superspeedway by far I've ever been on," Richard Petty said.

France was not moved.

"Anybody who wants to run can, and anybody who doesn't want to doesn't have to," said France, who took a few laps around the track at high speeds to prove his case that the speedway was raceable.

The day before the race, most of the "name" drivers, who had formed the Professional Drivers Association (PDA) about a month before the race to serve as the closest thing NASCAR would ever have to a union, declared their decision to boycott the race. As trucks hauling their race cars slowly pulled out of the speedway infield on Saturday, France was preparing the track for Sunday's race.

The transporter parade home—a day early—sparked some interest among fans who were traveling in the opposite direction toward the track. Some wondered if they had gotten their schedules crossed and missed the race.

The Talladega 500 was held as scheduled, although the field was a bare shadow of what it normally would have been. Thirteen Cup cars and 23 smaller Grand Touring racers—basically field fillers to make the starting grid bigger—participated. Bobby Isaac, one of the few major drivers who did not join the PDA, was the only driver with "star" quality in the field.

The race was won by Richard Brickhouse, a virtual unknown who originally joined the driver union but resigned before the Talladega event. Brickhouse, a farmer from Rocky Point, North Carolina, who was trying to ignite his racing career, never won again.

The race was run without incident, although strategically placed caution flags were a key to the lack to trouble.

Subsequent races at Talladega were run without tire controversies, generally because the tire manufacturers had more time to work on suitable compounds for the track. That was one of the drivers' main arguments in the first year—that the track had been rushed to completion and that the tire companies were pushed to prepare racing rubber for the first event.

Over the years, Talladega would become one of NASCAR's most popular destinations. Year One was soon forgotten.

66 Petty Rolls North

No one knew it then, of course, but when a raw-boned 21-year-old kid named Richard Petty first turned a lap in competition in what would become the Sprint Cup Series, he was beginning a journey that would end with 200 victories and 1,185 starts.

It was a long and winding trip that made him the King of NASCAR and one of international motorsports' most revered figures.

Where did this historic first step occur? Maybe at a short track in Petty's native North Carolina? At a historic NASCAR venue like Greenville-Pickens Speedway in South Carolina? At storied old Martinsville Speedway in Virginia? Uh, no. It was Toronto, Canada.

Petty made his first Sprint Cup run July 18, 1958, at the Canadian National Exposition Speedway, a .333-mile paved track near the shores of Lake Ontario in Toronto.

Petty finished 17th. He drove an Oldsmobile built in his father Lee's shop in Level Cross, North Carolina. Lee had run the car numerous times and sort of handed it down to his son.

In fact, Richard's fiercest competition in the Toronto event came from his father, who won the race on his way to winning the Sprint Cup title that season. Richard didn't finish the race—he was 17th of 19 cars—because he was spun out by an aggressive driver lapping cars.

That aggressive driver was Lee Petty, who gave no quarter to anyone, not even his son. Lee Petty was all about business. Every position meant more money to take home to keep the family enterprise afloat.

"Richard was all over the track," said Ross Kennedy, the flagman for the race. "Lee was leading and he came around and there was Richard in the way. Whomp—that was the end of Richard."

There was no grand design attached to Richard's Cup debut. He had raced for the first time in any sort of competition the previous week in a NASCAR Convertible Division race at Columbia Speedway in South Carolina. He raced in Toronto the next week simply because it was the next event on the NASCAR schedule.

Major-league racing ended at the Toronto track in 1967, and the site was eventually bulldozed. A soccer stadium now covers most of the property.

"When they tore the track down, somebody sent me a steel pole that the fence went on," Petty said. "So I have a souvenir of my first Cup race—a four-foot-high beam."

Petty vs. Petty

It isn't unusual for drivers to disagree with NASCAR decisions or dispute the results of races.

The latter doesn't happen that often these days because of the advent of computerized scoring. For many years, however, NASCAR scored races using a rudimentary paper approach that involved individuals recording each lap run by a driver on a scoresheet.

This often led to arguments between NASCAR officials and teams and between drivers and other drivers. And it sometimes led to official protests.

One of those occurred at Lakewood Speedway near Atlanta, Georgia, during the 1959 season. NASCAR champion Lee Petty protested the results after the race and demanded a recheck of the scorecards. During the process, errors were discovered and the win was awarded to Petty.

The driver who lost the win? Richard Petty, Lee's son. It would have been Richard's first Cup victory.

"It was just business," Richard said many years later.

Petty's first Cup car probably should be in a museum. No such luck on that. "I think I 'eliminated' it at Trenton," Petty said of a race at Trenton, New Jersey.

Some of the parts and pieces of that vehicle probably survive. It's just that the owners have no idea they're sitting on history.

67 A Guiding Hand

They have the best views in the house, but that opportunity comes with a hot seat.

They make up the spotter corps, the group of team owners, friends, former drivers, and other hangers-on who are responsible for "guiding" drivers through the smoke, fire, and trouble that often springs up during NASCAR races.

Spotters typically perch atop the highest building on the outside of the track. Each driver is required to have a spotter any time the team's car is on the track. Through radio communications, they attempt to guide drivers through crashes, alert them to potential on-track problems, and tell them when they've cleared traffic.

It's a tough job, one that some drivers prefer to fill with former drivers because they have a clear understanding of what's happening on the track.

Tim Fedewa, formerly a driver in the Nationwide Series, spots for Richard Petty Motorsports driver Marcos Ambrose. Fedewa won four times in the then-Busch Series in the late 1990s and 2000.

Fedewa walks the line between providing his driver with good information—but not too much information. "I'm very aware of trying to say too much," he said. "The way I explain it is that I'll give you information. I'm not telling you how to do it. I'm telling you what I see. You can take it and run with it or not.

"The past six or seven years or so, it's seemed like the drivers want more information. That's a change. It used to be that they didn't want so much. The younger kids now are searching for information. They want to know everything."

Spotters also "escort" their drivers along pit road, helping them find their spot during crowded stops and reminding them to avoid speeding penalties as they enter and leave the pits (pit-road speeds differ at each track).

A good spotter can make the difference between winning and losing.

68 Suitcase Jake

The crew chief who led Dale Earnhardt Sr. to his first Sprint Cup victory in 1979 didn't stay with the future champion for his years of dominance in the sport.

Jake Elder, one of the best mechanical minds in the history of NASCAR, helped to jump-start Earnhardt's big-time career as the rough and ragged driver arrived at stock car racing's top level after years of driving on hardscrabble Southern short tracks.

Earnhardt crossed the finish line first for the first time April 1, 1979, at Bristol, Tennessee. Elder, who saw a champion's foundation in Earnhardt's still-rough demeanor, was along for the ride.

That victory produced one of the best quotes in NASCAR history. After the race win, Elder told Earnhardt, "Stick with me, kid, and we'll have diamonds as big as horse turds."

This won't surprise anyone who later came into contact with Elder, but he was the one who didn't "stick." Elder left the Earnhardt team the next season (which became Earnhardt's first championship year) for what he assumed would be greener pastures.

It was a process Elder, who died in February 2010 at the age of 73, would repeat many times during a career that saw him in more jobs than a normal resume sheet could hold. His frequent job-hopping earned him the nickname Suitcase Jake. Virtually everyone in NASCAR circles knew him by that name.

If Elder soured on a situation, he would pack his tools and head down the road, sometimes with only a moment's notice. He always assumed that the next thing—whatever it was—would be better.

"I have a problem getting people to understand how I want things done," Elder once said. "Usually, I can get it done myself quicker than I can explain to them how I want it done."

Elder, whose success in stock car racing could be linked to his expertise in developing winning chassis combinations, started work at Petty Enterprises in the late 1950s. He made a name for himself in the 1960s while working for the giant Holman-Moody Ford factory team based in Charlotte, North Carolina.

Elder and driver David Pearson were both rising quickly through the sport during that period, and they teamed at Holman-Moody to win 27 races and the national championship in 1968 and '69, seasons in which Pearson started 48 and 51 races. The toughest competition during that period came from Elder's former employer, Petty Enterprises, and its lead driver, Richard Petty.

While at Holman-Moody, Elder also led Mario Andretti, one of the world's best racers but an infrequent visitor to NASCAR, to victory in the 1967 Daytona 500. It was Andretti's only win in NASCAR in 14 appearances.

In the early 1970s, Elder hooked up with young driver Darrell Waltrip and was pit boss for Waltrip's first Cup victory at Nashville, Tennessee, in 1975.

"He could hook up whatever horsepower they had to a chassis and make it work," longtime NASCAR broadcaster Barney Hall said. "He knew what made the cars work underneath. Teams would see him coming down pit road and let the jacks down on their cars because they knew he could take a glance at the springs and know what they had.

"And he was a man of few words. I remember several radio interviews with him after his car fell out of a race. Somebody would ask him what happened, and he'd say, 'Blowed up,' and walk off."

As racing got bigger, more impersonal, and more sophisticated in the 1990s, old-timers like Elder often were passed by as engineers and specialists began to dominate the sport's shops. Late in his career, he moved away from high-level responsibilities and worked as a team mechanic and in various other jobs.

He always had the "suitcase" at the ready.

69 The Very Big Ones

In NASCAR, there are wrecks, and then there are *wrecks*. Virtually every race has at least one or two spinouts, multi-car incidents, blown tires, or blown engines.

But some accidents are so huge that they raise questions. How do people survive them? And why do those people return to the driver's seat time after time in the aftermath?

Some drivers do not survive crashes, of course. Dozens have died in on-track smashups during NASCAR's more than 60-year history—from names few people would recognize to one of the most famous of all time, Dale Earnhardt Sr.

But technological advances through the years have made race cars and race tracks much safer, and it is no longer surprising—in fact, it's almost expected—to see a driver flip a car multiple times or sail into a wall head-on at high speed and climb out of the vehicle unhurt.

Still, this is *big stuff*. Don't they think twice before climbing in again after rolling a car 10 times?

"I think as time goes on you become more and more immune to it as you go through big wrecks," Sprint Cup champion Jimmie Johnson said. "You build...I don't know if it's a false sense of security because it's still a dangerous sport, but you build a sense of security and understanding of situations and get better with it."

Johnson endured a spectacular crash in 2000 during a Nationwide (then Busch) Series race at Watkins Glen, New York. After a brake failure on the road course, his car sailed across open grass and a dirt surface before hitting foam barriers and slamming into a wall with tremendous force. The accident was one of the worst looking in series history, but Johnson was not injured.

"I was going 150 miles an hour on a downhill slope into a banked corner with no brakes," Johnson said. "I didn't know what was on the other side. I knew there were some tires there eventually [protecting the wall].

"It got really quiet. I got really calm. Once I realized I couldn't do anything, I kind of slumped over. It was the best thing I could do. It was an eerie, eerie feeling. I just kind of went numb and limp."

Ten years earlier in another Nationwide race, this time at Bristol Motor Speedway in Tennessee, Michael Waltrip almost met the end of his racing career—and his life. Waltrip's crash is remembered by many as the most vicious in NASCAR history, although undoubtedly there were many worse in the sport's building years in the 1950s when safety was often an afterthought and track conditions were primitive.

On April 7, 1990, Waltrip lost control of his car and hit the edge of a crossover gate at the high-banked Bristol track. The force of the full-speed crash caused Waltrip's car to explode, almost as if he had run over a bomb. Parts and pieces flew across the track, and the core of the car came to a sudden stop and dropped down the track banking.

Many spectators and pit onlookers—including Waltrip's older brother, Darrell, a veteran driver—feared the worst. There was no way Waltrip could have survived the crash, the thinking went, because his car had been transformed into a pile of mangled pieces. It wasn't even clear immediately where Waltrip was in the wreckage.

But Waltrip suddenly emerged from the remains of the car, having been protected by the safety cocoon around the driver's seat. He was not seriously injured.

"It was terrible, but yet I was okay," Waltrip said years later. "I was fine, so that gives you the mental leg up to go do it again. You forget immediately. As soon as you're back in the car, you're on it. I don't remember having any reservations about doing what I do. I just went and did it."

Thankfully, Waltrip has not had another wreck of that magnitude. In fact, few others have.

One of the most astounding wrecks in recent years occurred in April 2009 at Talladega Superspeedway, a 2.66-mile track that has been a magnet for spectacular accidents. This one was almost too spectacular.

Racing for the win in the frontstretch trioval on the last lap, Brad Keselowski made contact with the car of Carl Edwards, punting Edwards' Ford into the air, into the grandstand fence, and almost into the crowd. Parts from the accident flew into the stands and injured several fans.

Edwards wasn't hurt, except by the fact that Keselowski won the race. Edwards climbed from his battered car and jokingly ran on foot across the line to "finish" the race.

Could That Be Blood?

Oppressive heat has been a problem inside NASCAR race cars since the sport's very beginnings. Numerous tactics and devices have been used over the years to battle the elements. Forced-air cooling systems in current Cup cars perform well, but the driver really suffers when those fail.

Drivers have carried various cool fluids in their race cars over the years as a way to fight the heat. One of those drivers—pioneer Buck Baker—caused a brief scare with his race-day drink of choice in the 1950 Southern 500 at Darlington (South Carolina) Raceway.

When the marathon event started, Baker had a bottle of cold tomato juice inside his car. Baker was involved in one of several crashes that day. The bottle broke and splashed the juice on his head.

He wasn't seriously injured, but the shock of the safety workers who were the first on the crash scene can be imagined.

"It's funny—you forget about those wrecks that quick and then you go do the same stupid stuff again and again—at least I do," Edwards said. "So, I'd say that it's far from my mind. One of the things that attracted me to racing so much was that the first time I drove a race car it scared the hell out of me. I was like, 'Man, that's pretty exciting.'

"Now, I don't get that feeling. It's just the competition, and the fear is losing. That's the only real fear out there—making a mistake that costs you a position or the race.

"You have to learn from the wrecks and react right up to the point where you slow down the race car. You can't do that. You can't slow down or be less competitive. The fact is that you have to go back and race and do the best you can. Fortunately, it's a lot safer than bull riding or motocross racing. You can walk away."

At least most of the time you can.

Three years before Edwards' big crash, Jeff Gordon endured a huge one of his own at the super-fast Pocono Raceway. His brakes failed at the end of the track's long front straightaway where speeds are fastest, and he endured one of the hardest hits of his racing career.

"It definitely rung my bell really good," Gordon said. "My first instinct was to put it in first gear to slow it down, maybe spin it around. I hit really hard. I was really loopy. But, from the mental impact, it was no big deal. What crossed my mind was what can we do to try to help in every one of those crashes. Obviously, we have a different brake package now at Pocono.

"It's like everything—a win or a wreck. It's a learning process that you try to put in your memory bank and say, 'Okay, how can I do it better next time?' If you had to go right back out there the next lap and do it again, then, yeah, you're probably going to be a little gun-shy. But you make laps, you race for several weeks, and your instincts are back as a race car driver."

For Michael Waltrip, who is reminded of his brutal Bristol crash virtually every week, his immediate return to driving included the thought that he already had been through the worst.

"I just thought I could never have a wreck like that again," Waltrip said. "And I haven't. I just said to the Lord that he didn't want me to be famous for having the worst wreck ever and that be the end of it. I was able to get through that somehow and go on to win races and have a lot of fun over the years that followed that."

70 Rocky Mountain High

The vast majority of teams involved in NASCAR's three major series—Sprint Cup, Nationwide, and Camping World Truck—planted their shops within a 75-mile radius of Charlotte, North Carolina.

Most of the sport's parts suppliers, engineering companies, and support systems also are in or around Charlotte, and the Charlotte area also is home to one of NASCAR's legendary tracks—Charlotte Motor Speedway (which actually is located in Concord, North Carolina). Charlotte, recognized as one of the birthplaces of the sport, also is the location of the new NASCAR Hall of Fame.

It might be somewhat of a surprise, then, to discover that there is a Sprint Cup team based in Denver—not Denver, North Carolina, but Denver, Colorado.

Furniture Row Racing did not open in Colorado to avoid one of the problems sometimes associated with teams in the Charlotte area—the easy movement of employees and information. In and around Charlotte, mechanics and pit crew members can hop from team to team and job to job with relative ease, and "secrets" developed by one team seldom stay there as employees bounce around.

Furniture Row, isolated near the Rocky Mountains, doesn't have these problems. But it is where it is because team owner Barney Visser, who also owns the Furniture Row home furnishings chain, lives in Denver. When Visser started a team in 2005, he figured he might as well park it close to home.

This makes for an interesting situation, to say the least. Travel is significantly different for Furniture Row team members. Team transporters roll out of Charlotte every week for track locations in the Southeast, Midwest, and beyond. It's a different spin for Furniture Row trucks.

Parts used by Furniture Row often are created in the Charlotte area, and that presents an unusual scenario. Furniture Row the business sends a truck across the country every week carrying furniture and other items. The racing team takes advantage of this situation by asking the furniture truckers to toss a few racing parts into the mix.

So the engine that does well in a race one week in Daytona might have been delivered alongside a sofa.

Although many of the mechanics, engine builders, and other racing specialists who work for NASCAR teams live in the Carolinas, Furniture Row competition director Mark McArdle said the Denver team has no trouble recruiting experienced team members to Colorado.

"Most of the guys who are working for us are originally members of other organizations in North Carolina," McArdle said. "One of the guys in the shop calls us the John Madden Oakland Raiders—the guys everybody else kicked out and we're going to come back and win a championship."

Excellent skiing, fishing, and hunting opportunities in and near the Rockies attract team members, as does Rocky Mountain National Park. It's not difficult to fall in love with the Rockies environment.

Furniture Row makes it easier for employees to deal with the time-zone differences by scheduling its workday from 6:00 AM to 3:00 PM. The hours coincide with typical workday hours in the Eastern time zone, making contact with suppliers, vendors, and other teams in and near Charlotte simple.

Furniture Row has an engineering alliance with Richard Childress Racing, and the Stewart-Haas Racing team trains and employs the crew that pits the No. 78 Chevrolet.

Does it all work? Yes. There was proof positive in May 2011 when Furniture Row driver Regan Smith outran the odds and won the Southern 500 at Darlington Raceway in South Carolina. It was Furniture Row's breakthrough victory, and it came in one of the season's most difficult races. It was no fluke.

Other teams didn't immediately move to Colorado, but Smith's win demonstrated that teams outside the Charlotte circle can survive. And even thrive.

71 Indianapolis Motor Speedway

For the vast majority of its century of existence, Indianapolis Motor Speedway was home to one major event—the Indianapolis 500, a race famous the world over. Everybody who cared anything about motorsports circled the month of May on their calendars and anticipated 500 wild miles of open-wheel competition at Indy.

There was occasional talk of adding a NASCAR event to the IMS schedule, but the discussions didn't reach a serious level until the 1990s, when NASCAR's second generation of leadership—Bill France Jr.—took advantage of his sport's increasing popularity to close a deal with then-IMS kingpin Tony George. NASCAR would go to Indy in 1994.

It was one of the most significant decisions in NASCAR history. Stock cars would leave their tire tracks on the surface of the most famous speedplant in the world, and much of the sporting world would take note.

Tom Weisenbach, former national sales manager at IMS, said the NASCAR race "has helped solidify the speedway as literally the leader in international motorsports. And it opened a lot of doors for the France family, which was trying to build NASCAR nationally. I think that was a critical point for NASCAR. It's almost hallowed ground."

Jeff Gordon, a former Indiana resident, won the first Brickyard 400 in 1994 before a packed house, and the race was off and running. Slowly, many of the traditionalists who scoffed at the idea of Indy hosting anything other than the Indianapolis 500—several were quite vocal in their opposition—were won over.

Andy Graves, now a key at-track official in Toyota's NASCAR program, was team manager for Juan Pablo Montoya when

Montoya won the Indy 500 in 2000. Graves has seen Indy from both sides.

"I know what Indy means to open-wheel racers," Graves said. "It's still extremely special. It's definitely more electrifying than when we go there as NASCAR. It still gives me chills, regardless of which series I'm in, to stand there on the grid right before the start and to see grandstands on both sides packed. As far as you can see, all you can see is people. It's very special. I guess it's hard to put into words exactly what that means.

"I knew NASCAR going there was going to be controversial at first, but at the end of the day, it's been huge for both sides. And I think it's really great for racing in North America in general."

The 100th anniversary of the Indianapolis 500 was celebrated in May 2011. The race was the 95th in the series, the track having been shuttered to racing during parts of the two world wars. The first 500 was held in 1911, 37 years before NASCAR was born.

Although NASCAR racing has been more popular than Indy-style competition for many years, the 500 still rules IMS. Practice, qualifying and competition at the 500 stretch over weeks, while NASCAR's annual visit is limited to a weekend. And Indy's layout is much more attuned to open-wheel racing.

"The 500 is still the linchpin of the place," said John Cooper, a retired motorsports executive who was IMS president from 1979 to 1983. "The crowds are about the same in size, but you can't take away nearly 100 years of history."

NASCAR crowd sizes at Indy have been down in recent seasons, but the circuit's annual visit to the track remains a seasonal highlight.

72 Monumental Undertakings

One of the most-visited spots on the giant piece of Florida real estate where Bill France Sr. built his classic speedway, Daytona International Speedway, in 1959 is not near the racing surface or in the grandstands or in the track's massive infield.

It's outside the front gates between the speedway entrances and International Speedway Boulevard, which fronts the track. Thousands stop by—the numbers obviously are much larger during race weeks—every month to remember and to reflect and to take photographs.

The spot contains a 9' bronze statue of seven-time Sprint Cup champion Dale Earnhardt Sr., one of stock car racing's all-time most popular drivers. Earnhardt died in the fourth turn at Daytona in February 2001, and the statue was unveiled outside the speedway February 8, 2002.

In the statue, Earnhardt is holding the 1998 Daytona 500 trophy in his right hand and is raising his left hand to the sky in celebration. The statue's plaza also includes two bronzed driving gloves and a penny that represents the good-luck coin a 9-year-old girl gave Earnhardt the morning of the '98 race. Earnhardt mounted the original penny to his dash that day.

Although perhaps the most famous, the Earnhardt statue is not the only one showcased at speedways.

At Atlanta Motor Speedway, a large bronze statue on a granite base honors seven-time Cup champion Richard Petty, the series' winningest driver. The statue shows Petty, appropriately wearing a cowboy hat and sunglasses, signing his autograph for a young fan. It was dedicated in November 1992 on the last weekend of Petty's driving career. His last race was at AMS.

Fans look up at a statue of Dale Earnhardt in front of Daytona International Speedway in Daytona Beach, Florida, on Wednesday, February 16, 2011.
(AP Photo/Lynne Sladky)

Also located outside the gates of Daytona International Speedway is a monument honoring NASCAR founder Bill France Sr. and his wife, Anne. France founded NASCAR in Daytona Beach in 1947, and Anne was very involved in the organization's operations.

The statue on display at Dover International Speedway can claim to be one of the biggest in sports. "Miles the Monster," a 46' fiberglass beast, is depicted "bursting" out of the ground outside the speedway gates. Named to match the speedway's "Monster Mile" nickname, Miles has glowing red eyes and is so huge he holds a full-size race car in his right hand.

73 Some Hard-Earned Publicity

NASCAR founder Bill France Sr. was starving for publicity for his new racing enterprise in the 1950s. With the formation of NASCAR in 1947, France had managed to corral many drivers, car owners, and tracks into a mostly cohesive unit after years of ragtag, unorganized racing.

But France faced a long, hard road in convincing newspapers, magazines, and electronic media that his fledgling racing organization was the real thing—and that it deserved steady, level coverage. He often returned to Daytona Beach empty-handed after meeting with newspaper sports editors and trying to sell his brand.

So it might be assumed to have been a good thing in 1956 when NASCAR got a giant, multi-photograph splash in *Life* magazine, then one of the most respected and widely circulated magazines in the country.

Russ Truelove, however, might argue with that position. Having read about the NASCAR races on the hard-packed sand of the Daytona Beach shore in 1956, Truelove drove south from his home in Waterbury, Connecticut, with the idea of participating. He worked as the service manager at a Lincoln-Mercury dealership, and he drove to Daytona in a new Mercury hardtop he had purchased there, planning to race it on the beach. It was normal in those days for drivers to race their street vehicles. Before Truelove left home, he painted a number on the sides of the car and installed a roll bar.

Truelove made the field for the race and wasn't shy about running hard once the green flag flew. But trouble came early.

He tried to pass Jim Reed as they neared the course's north turn, but the Mercury got caught in the soft sand in the turn, and the front wheels dug in. The car started fishtailing and flipped into the air, creating one of the most spectacular accidents in the history of racing on the beach course. And there have been many.

Photos of Truelove's wreck were spread across the pages of *Life*, and readers who had never heard of NASCAR or who had only vague knowledge of stock car racing suddenly saw what these daredevil drivers experienced.

Meanwhile, Truelove, who now spends part of the winter in Daytona reliving the old days with a new generation of racing fans, had lost his ride home. But he ran into some good fortune. A man from Hartford, Connecticut, was in Daytona repossessing cars and offered Truelove a ride home in one.

He survived to race another day.

74 Not So Strictly Stock

When Bill France Sr. founded NASCAR, his idea of a successful motorsports series had one thing at its heart—the American-made street automobile.

That's why France named his spotlighted series, the one that first cranked engines in 1949, Strictly Stock. The plan was to race automobiles virtually identical to those people drove on Main Street and parked in their driveways. France understood the attraction of open-wheel racing, but he felt certain that Americans would relate to daredevil drivers racing Chevrolets and Fords, the same vehicles that were being sold by the thousands in the post-World War II era on speedways across the land.

He was right.

Before the arrival of the Strictly Stock Series, most racing that involved stock cars was for "jalopies," which usually were 1930s-era American-made coupes rescued from junkyards and radically rebuilt. Raced on dirt tracks in conditions that often were horrendous, the cars were covered with dirt after only a few laps, and their exteriors were slammed by rocks flying off the track and by rival drivers plowing into them.

The 1939 Ford Coupe was a popular model picked by racers. *Speed Age*, a widely distributed racing magazine during the sport's early years, suggested that drivers remove inside door handles and window cranks from the cars because "all of these items are aimed directly at you when you are flipping, so they cannot harm you if they are not there."

France took the "jalopy" platform and lifted it to another level. Instead of junk cars being converted into race cars, France wanted to take new cars off showroom floors and throw them into competition. It was "showroom shine," not junkyard grime.

He announced the first Strictly Stock race for Charlotte (North Carolina) Speedway on June 19, 1949, and had no shortage of entries. Most of the drivers planning to participate in the race drove their street cars to the event and then raced them. When the green flag flew, Buick Roadmasters, Oldsmobile 88s, Lincolns, Fords—nine makes in all—roared into the first turn in a cloud of dust.

Of course, they were not "strictly" stock. But they were close. Drivers used safety enhancements like airplane safety belts and inexpensive hardware-store cords to tie across their laps. At least one driver wrapped himself in a truck-tire inner tube. Owners put tape over headlights and grilles to provide a little protection against rocks flying from the rutted racing surface.

After a few races, it became clear that cars could not be raced in "showroom" form. The track surfaces were too punishing, and the races were too long.

One of the first areas to be addressed was wheel strength. Wheels broke repeatedly under the pressure of rough track surfaces and heavy cars barreling into the turns.

"The wheels got better after a few races," pioneer driver Buck Baker said. "We had to make double-plated wheels. I used to cut the center out of one and put it in another one to strengthen it. Everybody did things like that."

Steering wheels occasionally broke, too. Baker responded to that dilemma in a race at Charlotte in the 1950s. "I drove with a pair of vise grips the rest of the race," he said. "I already had them in the car, so I just clamped down on the column and turned it with the grips. It didn't go as fast as normal, but I finished the race." Like some other races in which he battled ill-handling cars, Baker finished that one with bloody hands.

The Biggest Blowout

Finally, it seemed, Dale Earnhardt was going to put an end to the Daytona 500 jinx that had followed him his entire career. Although he had accomplished virtually everything else that might be expected of a star stock car racer, Earnhardt had not won his sport's biggest race.

That sour streak appeared to be ending in the 1990 Daytona 500. Earnhardt led 155 laps and had a comfortable lead over Derrike Cope as they took the white flag. Then the demons of the race slapped Earnhardt in the face once more. He ran over debris on the last lap and blew a tire entering the third turn.

Cope passed him easily and won the race.

The mangled tire wound up in the shop—and later the museum—of Earnhardt's team owner, Richard Childress. Earnhardt finally won the 500 eight years later.

As the tough nature of racing became obvious, car companies became involved, producing "high performance" parts for race cars. Some were sold as "severe usage" kits.

Among the first big safety additions was the development of roll bars, which were designed to support a car's roof in case of a rollover. In the first years, some drivers rejected the advance because the bars added weight to the cars, but NASCAR eventually made them mandatory. Later, roll cages, covering virtually the entire interior of the car, replaced the bars.

Originally, cars raced with street tires, but Goodyear joined the sport in 1954 and began working on specialty tires for events. "Skinny" street tires proved to have a footprint far too small for heavy, fast cars.

In the 1960s, teams moved away from street cars and toward vehicles that were specifically built for racing.

After numerous driver deaths in the early 1960s, engineers developed the rubber fuel cell, a bladder-type device placed inside cars' fuel tanks to lessen the possibility of gas spillage in crashes.

Driver uniforms made from flameproof material and car fire extinguisher systems followed.

As racing got bigger and moved onto new, faster speedways, aerodynamic research and engine development produced radical changes in the cars, and France's idea of "strictly stock" faded steadily into the background.

In 1987, Bill Elliott pushed one of the strongest of those purpose-built cars to the fastest qualifying speed—212.809 mph—in NASCAR history. That run came at Talladega Superspeedway in Alabama, and rapidly increasing speeds and airborne, flipping race cars eventually led NASCAR to clamp restrictor plates on engines, limiting speeds at Talladega and Daytona International Speedway, then the circuit's two fastest tracks.

In 1989, Goodyear changed the NASCAR landscape dramatically by introducing radial tires to the top stock car series. The new tires, which replaced the bias-ply tires that had been used since NASCAR's early years, were used at Cup short tracks in 1990 and soon became universal at all tracks. The radials were more durable and dependable, but they changed the "feel" of racing for drivers dramatically, requiring drivers and teams to reassess their tire strategies. The transition also was very difficult for some drivers, particularly those who had been in the sport a long time.

The sport's next major changes came after a series of deaths rocked NASCAR in 2000 and 2001. Drivers Adam Petty, Kenny Irwin Jr., Tony Roper, and Dale Earnhardt Sr. were killed in crashes, and Earnhardt's death, in particular, put safety development into high gear.

Among the results—a new race car. Called the Car of Tomorrow, it debuted at Bristol Motor Speedway in March 2007 and became the Cup series' full-time car in 2008. The COT was taller and wider than the previous racing models, had a large rear-deck wing and had a new interior, a space that had been changed most significantly by the movement of the driver's seat 4" closer to the center of the car.

Safety advances also included mandatory use of head-and-neck restraints designed primarily to combat the often fatal "neck whipping" injuries suffered in head-on crashes, and the use of SAFER barriers, so-called "soft walls" that made impact into track walls much safer.

Over the course of 60-plus years, the cars and tracks of NASCAR changed dramatically, moving Bill France's "strictly stock" vision into new territory.

75 A 14-Lap Victory?

Modern-day NASCAR fans are used to seeing races conclude with two or more drivers grappling for the win at the finish line with their cars separated by bare fractions of a second.

The margin of victory in the 2011 Daytona 500, for example, was only .118 of a second as Trevor Bayne edged Carl Edwards. Later in that season, eight cars swept across the finish line in a tight group at Talladega Superspeedway at the end of the Aaron's 499 as Jimmie Johnson nipped Clint Bowyer by .002 of a second for the win.

Blink your eyes, and you miss it.

It might amaze many to learn, then, that two-time Cup champion Ned Jarrett once won a race by 14 laps. Not 14 seconds—14 *laps*. It was almost like Jarrett was a calendar page ahead of everyone else.

It happened in the 1965 Southern 500 at Darlington Raceway in South Carolina. In those days, the Southern 500 was run on

That Was Really Close

The May 16, 1993, Sprint Cup race at Infineon Raceway in Sonoma, California, was not particularly noteworthy for its finish—Geoff Bodine beat Ernie Irvan to the checkered flag—but it was a landmark event for NASCAR.

For the first time in Cup racing, electronic scoring was used. At the race finish, teams, news media, officials, and fans knew immediately that Bodine had won the race by .53 of a second over Irvan. The numbers flashed on video monitors as each car completed the race.

This opened the door not only for more accurate timing and scoring throughout races but also for a fast way to compare finishes over the years and rank them. NASCAR had experienced plenty of tight finishes over the years, but there had been no concrete way to compare them. To listen to longtime drivers talk, dozens of races finished with the winner a fraction of an inch in front of second place, but there was no accurate way to make a measurement.

The system has been refined over the years, and now numbers fly across monitors with every lap at a Cup race, and each driver's deficit to the race leader is immediately known.

Since electronic scoring began, the two closest finishes in Cup racing each found the winner out front by a microscopic .002 of a second.

Ricky Craven edged Kurt Busch to win at Darlington Raceway in a fender-banging, side-by-side finish in 2003.

Jimmie Johnson matched that number April 17, 2011, at Talladega Superspeedway when he led an eight-car sweep to the finish line and beat Clint Bowyer by .002.

Labor Day, and conditions typically were hot and humid. Drivers often finished the race—those who did complete all 500 miles, that is—with tongues hanging out, sweat soaking their firesuits, and the stress and strain of the day clearly written across their faces.

It was the same on September 6, 1965, and cars were overheating right and left during the grueling race. Seven drivers dropped out of the event with engine trouble, and several others parked with gasket failures and the like.

But Jarrett rolled on throughout the long afternoon, trying to pamper his Ford and keep it from succumbing to the conditions. He went fast enough to stay out front but slow enough to survive.

The veteran driver—he would retire the following season—came into the event with some extra support.

"Bob Colvin [Darlington track official] had asked me to speak to his Methodist youth group on Sunday night before the race, and I asked for their prayers," Jarrett said. "I went away with a genuine feeling that I had their support. The next day I was on pit road, and a gentleman walked up to me and introduced himself as a minister from Orangeburg, South Carolina.

"He told me that he had talked to Fireball Roberts before the race in 1958 and told him he felt like he was going to win, and he did. He said that he had the same feeling about me that day, and he wanted me to know that his prayers were with me. I was on cloud nine. I went into the race with a tremendous amount of confidence."

At day's end, as matters turned out, Jarrett was carrying an overload of confidence. He took the checkered flag 14 laps in front of second-place Buck Baker and 19 laps ahead of third-place Darel Dieringer and fourth-place Roy Mayne.

Jarrett said he was not aware of the staggering size of his lead over the closing laps, although he knew he was in pretty good shape.

Jarrett's margin of victory is the largest in NASCAR history—and that isn't likely to change.

76 A Ghostly Track

Dozens of former speedways that once heard the roar of engines—NASCAR and otherwise—no longer exist. Some couldn't attract the crowds necessary to pay purses. Others were built in locations where the land eventually became more valuable for other business pursuits. And others couldn't keep up with the advances of the times and were left along the trail as racing sped ahead.

Few former NASCAR tracks have a story as riveting as that of Memphis-Arkansas Speedway, however.

The track was a strange animal—a 1.5-mile, high-banked dirt oval. It was built in Lehi, Arkansas, 14 miles from the Mississippi River in what was once—and now is again—fertile farmland.

The speedway ran Sprint Cup (then Grand National) races from 1954 to 1957 and, because of its length and severe banking was one of NASCAR's earliest examples of high-speed, high-risk racing. It was too fast and too dangerous for the technology of the '50s, and drivers showing up to compete at the track realized the difficulties immediately.

It was one of the few tracks that shot a sense of fear through drivers in those barnstorming early days of NASCAR.

"That track was something," NASCAR pioneer driver Cotton Owens said. "It was rough, and you got through the turns the best way you could. It had so many holes. It was so dusty you couldn't see."

The first race was held October 10, 1954, and the trouble the track could produce showed its ugly face quickly. Four drivers and two crewmen were hospitalized after incidents during the race. One of the area newspapers described the race as full of "wrecks, gasoline explosions, and flaming cars." Among the injured was a mechanic who was burned badly in a pit fire.

A sad trend had been established.

In another race at the track on October 9, 1955, driver Tiny Lund, making his first start in the Cup series, was involved in a brutal accident—one that could have been much worse. Lund was thrown from his Chevrolet when the car flipped several times. He landed on the track surface, and drivers behind him swerved to avoid him. Ralph Liguori hit Lund's helmet as he drove through the wreckage.

"He came out of the car, and I ran over him," Liguori said. "I thought I had killed him. I got word he was alive and conscious. When I went to the hospital to see him that night, he said, 'What happened? I heard you ran over me. How come?' I said, 'Well, I thought you were dead, so I wasn't going to swerve to miss you.'"

Remarkably, Lund suffered only a broken arm and a few bruises.

"The track was really, really fast for dirt," Richard Petty remembered. "And it got rough. We'd never run a mile and a half on dirt and never anything close to that fast. Cars would go into the turns and just start hitting each other.

"I was there when Tiny got thrown out of the car in the middle of the track. He was as big as a car. He was laying there with his T-shirt and white pants on in that dark gumbo [soil]."

Lund's all-white clothing probably saved his life, allowing drivers to see him more easily in the dust that flew around the track.

Former driver Johnny Allen said the Memphis-Arkansas track was very difficult to drive. "There were ruts in the track," Allen said. "There was so much dust you could barely see. You were going a hundred miles an hour into the corner full of ruts and big holes. You had to grit your teeth and hope there wasn't anybody in the middle of it."

After flirting with the devil, the track claimed lives in June 1956.

Clint McHugh, a 28-year-old driver attempting to qualify for his first Cup race, shot through the railing at the top of the banking in Turn 3, flipped down the bank on the outside of the track, and landed in a small lake. Three observers jumped into the water to remove McHugh from the car, but he died on the way to a local hospital, having suffered two broken legs, a head wound, and other injuries.

The next day—race day—saw the death of 27-year-old driver Thomas "Cotton" Priddy. Priddy hit Paul Goldsmith's car and then flipped down the track. He was thrown from the car as it soared 15' into the air, and his body was hit by cars as heavy dust obscured the view of the accident scene.

"I'm a God-fearing woman, and he was a God-fearing man," Priddy's wife told newspaper reporters later. "Now he's been turned over to the hands of the Lord."

Among the drivers who had the misfortune of flying out of the Lehi track was three-time NASCAR champion Lee Petty, whose car popped out near the first turn and landed in the lake outside the facility. He was not seriously injured. The "floating" car survived—sort of. Its future was humble. It was converted into a street car for Richard, Lee's son and future Cup driver.

The track's final race was held in 1957, and according to newspaper reports, many in the crowd of 10,000 left the track before the race's halfway point because of excessive dust.

The track's owners struggled with financial problems—both at the track and elsewhere. It was sold in 1957, and the land was returned to rice farming.

Visitors to the area today can see the shape of the track still imprinted on the land, and there are pieces remaining of the main grandstand.

But it's silent. No engine noise.

77 Catch Him If You Can

A longstanding figure on NASCAR pit roads wandered off into the sunset in the 2011 season. His position was mostly underappreciated and seldom noticed unless his job—literally—went up in flames. The catch-can man was discarded by NASCAR in 2011 when changes in how race cars are refueled made the pit-crew position unnecessary.

For decades, the catch-can man, a position on every pit crew, stood at the rear of cars during pit stops, holding a small can to an overflow vent to "catch" the fuel overflow when the crew's gasman refueled the car.

In 2011, NASCAR switched to self-venting fuel cans, eliminating the need for the catch-can man and dropping the number of over-the-wall pit crew people from seven to six. The system had been field-tested in the Camping World Truck Series.

The process wasn't as simple as replacing a man with a device, however. Pit stops at the start of the 2011 season were a little slower as teams adjusted to the change, and the situation involved more than fueling. Most teams also used the catch-can man to make track-bar and wedge adjustments at the rear of the car during stops. Those responsibilities were handed over to the rear-tire carrier (in most cases) after the change.

"Now we won't be dumping [fuel] as fast as we were," Joe Gibbs Racing crew chief Greg Zipadelli said. "We'll have to pick speed up in the tiny details. We'll be relying solely on the gasman for a lot of things.

"With the catch-can man gone, we can't ask too much of the other people. The track bar and rear wedge adjustments are big parts of our adjustments during a race, and the catch-can man did that without affecting anybody else."

Although the change had serious impact on the way pit crews operate during stops, it came along with a key positive. The catch-can man, standing at the rear of the car, generally was the most vulnerable member of the pit crew.

One of the most serious pit-road accidents in NASCAR history involved a catch-can man. Don Miller, who later would become president of Penske Racing, was seriously injured while working as catch-can man for driver Gary Bettenhausen at Talladega Superspeedway in 1974. During pit stops, a car driven by Grant Adcox spun and slid into the rear of the Bettenhausen car, trapping Miller between the two vehicles. Among the injuries he sustained were a broken back, a broken pelvis, and two crushed legs.

Miller, now retired, recovered to return to the team after numerous surgeries.

The 2011 change was difficult for some teams to handle. Pit-stop times ballooned in some cases, leading to changes among over-the-wall personnel. With passing often tough on the track, those fractions of seconds on pit road became even more important.

78 How Young Is Too Young?

Kurt Busch jumped into NASCAR racing and showed right away that he had the stuff to be a winner. He had four victories in 2000—his rookie season—in the Camping World Truck Series and quickly moved up to Sprint Cup, where he won four times in 2002 and 2003 and then won the championship in 2004.

Clearly, Busch had the right stuff. But Busch had a warning for everybody, as in, "You ain't seen nothing yet. Wait 'til you see my brother race," he said.

Kyle Busch, seven years Kurt's junior, rolled into NASCAR behind his brother and indeed made a name for himself rapidly.

As early as his pre-teen years, Kyle had targeted the top level of stock car racing. Under the direction of his father, Tom, Kyle followed in Kurt's tire tracks, winning go-cart titles and then succeeding at short tracks in and around their hometown of Las Vegas.

Car owner Joe Gibbs (left) talks with his driver Kyle Busch before qualifying for the Sylvania 300 NASCAR Sprint Cup Series auto race at New Hampshire Motor Speedway on Friday, September 23, 2011, in Loudon, New Hampshire. (AP Photo/Jim Cole)

The Autograph Game

They can be seen at every NASCAR track—hundreds, often thousands of fans carrying photos, caps, diecast cars, and numerous other items linked to their favorite driver(s). They're all in search of one thing— the autograph.

Some leave the race track thrilled, their driver's signature emblazoned across his image. Most, though, never get close enough.

Although NASCAR drivers often are among the most accessible athletes in American professional sports, getting "face" time with them still can be very difficult. There are designated or traditional autograph spots located at many tracks on the schedule, but drivers choose whether or not they want to devote the time to signing autographs.

For the series' most popular drivers, the autograph is a troublesome part of the game. It isn't a difficult thing to do, signing your name. But when hundreds of people are standing across from you at a fence, all seeking the same thing, there is no way to accommodate everyone. And the first person who is left holding his item without an autograph sometimes is the first to become annoyed at a driver. It's not a win-win situation for drivers.

Where is the best place to get an autograph? Usually at a designated autograph-signing session. Drivers often appear at these at one of their sponsor's locations (a Lowe's store, for example) or at their souvenir trailer at the track.

Drivers also often sign autographs in the garage area at track locations, but corralling them to sign—even if you can get a garage pass—can be a difficult task. They're typically busy in the garage— this is their job, after all, and there often isn't time to sign dozens of autographs.

Drivers who sign in the garage have perfected the "walk-and-sign" procedure. Fans follow them as they walk from point A to point B, thrusting items toward them. The drivers walk as they sign. If they ever stop, they'll be encircled by the masses.

Having made his talents clear at a very early age, Kyle earned a ride in the Truck series at only 16—an age at which many teenagers are learning to drive on public roads. That moved him to faster tracks and in race fields with competitors much more experienced, but he did well, and he was on course to move into Sprint Cup racing, possibly before his 18th birthday.

Then NASCAR changed gears—and its rules. The sanctioning body decided that drivers younger than 18 could not race in any of its top three series—then called the Winston Cup Series, Busch Series, and Craftsman Truck Series.

Busch suddenly hit a roadblock. He had the talent. He didn't have the years.

Stalled by NASCAR, Busch joined the short-track American Speed Association Late Model series in 2002 and raced out of the spotlight. It was important to keep racing somewhere, however. He wanted to keep growing and moving—and moving fast.

"I felt like the whole world was taken from me and what I wanted I couldn't have any more," Busch said. "For me, being that young, I thought, 'I'm done, there's no more for me.' You're there and you get kicked out and you think, 'Well, who's going to want me now?'"

The negative turned into a positive, however. Busch gained valuable experience and was better situated to move into NASCAR two years later.

"Going to ASA and learning the things I was able to learn there about longer races, pit stops, strategy, this and that was really, really good for me instead of just driving the race car and have the crew chief make all the calls," Busch said. "I kind of have a sense of what I need to know about a race and how it plays out. Now if I was in the Cup series at 18, I would be lost. Completely lost."

Busch eventually moved into Nationwide and Cup racing and now is one of the best drivers in the sport. And he's still only in his mid-20s.

79 Riding to the Rescue

As NASCAR exploded in popularity in the early 1990s, stock car racing became a gravy train of sorts with almost everybody wanting to jump aboard. Sponsors were pouring millions of dollars into the sport, television networks were chasing bigger ratings with broadcasts of races, and ticket sales were soaring.

The tougher financial realities of the 2000s forced some new thinking in the boardrooms and shops of the sport, however, as bigger and better teams needed more and more money to keep top drivers in championship form. Sometimes it became necessary to look outside the sport, and that's where Rob Kauffman came in.

Kauffman is a billionaire. A mid-40s London-based investment firm co-owner, he also is an ardent motorsports enthusiast. And that enthusiasm was a very good thing for longtime NASCAR driver and relatively new team owner Michael Waltrip.

Waltrip jumped into serious team ownership in 2007, joining Toyota as it became a Sprint Cup competitor. But Waltrip's team struggled in the early going, and it quickly became clear that he needed more capital. Enter Kauffman, who put new cash into the team and became a co-owner.

Kauffman brushed up against the NASCAR world several years prior when he opened a classic-car restoration shop near Charlotte—he drives a restored 1970 Plymouth Superbird—and ran into people who suggested he might invest some of his money in stock car racing.

"It's not a matter of throwing money at it or finding the secret sauce," Kauffman said. "I think it's a matter of getting people to work better together. With this sort of racing, you can't make any mistakes. It's a split-second business. No mistakes on pit road. No bad calls. And you have to have a little luck. It's a combination of things across the board. There's not one magic switch you flip.

"This has been an interesting ride. We buy companies and try to fix them up. I was a little surprised at how big a business this really was. It was a bigger mouthful than I anticipated. But so far so good.

"It's a great sport. It's a mediocre business at this point. I'm optimistic that it will become a less mediocre business, but it's a great sport."

Although he likes to be "Basic Rob," not the rich guy who showed up suddenly, Kauffman necessarily travels in significant circles. The people he meets, he says, have great respect for NASCAR and for the competition it produces.

"After Formula One, this is probably the No. 1 form of racing on the planet," he said. "There's extreme interest in it globally. A lot of people look at NASCAR from the outside and are in awe of how big and how exciting it is.

"I think it's easier to criticize this when you're on the inside, but from the outside, it's pretty impressive not only as a sport but also as a business."

80 When a Winner's Not a Winner

Everything isn't always as it seems in NASCAR racing. For example, you can "win" a race and not win it.

Johnny Allen was the very first example of that in the history of Bristol Motor Speedway, which ran its first Sprint Cup (then Grand National) race in 1961. It was a hot day in the middle of the Tennessee summer, and the Bristol track, now one of the behe-moths of NASCAR with seating for more than 160,000, opened with about 18,000 seats in rows of concrete stands. At its opening, the track was known as Bristol International Speedway.

The first race was a big event in the mountains of eastern Tennessee, but drivers knew when they showed up that the heat and humidity would have a big impact on the day's almost-four-hour run. Although modern stock cars have cooling systems that cut the impact of high temperatures, there was very little teams could do in racing's early years to help a roasting driver.

Nowhere was the damaging effect of the heat that day at Bristol felt more than in the cockpit of Jack Smith's No. 46 Pontiac, which started 12th in the race but had the lead by lap 151. The floorboard was blistering hot very early in the race, leading Smith, a bulldog of a man who was one of the toughest drivers ever to sit in a race car, to ponder exiting the vehicle before the race had reached its halfway point.

In an interview years later, Smith remembered that the cir-cumstances—his right foot was taking most of the force of the heat—meant that he couldn't possibly finish the race.

Fortunately for Smith, Allen, one of his closest friends on the circuit, had dropped out of the race earlier in the day. Oddly, heat—but of a very different sort—had sidelined Allen's Chevrolet 106 laps into the race.

"I burned the rear end up on the car and came in the pits," Allen said. "They jacked the car up and pulled the rear end out and were going to put another one in and get me back out because it was so early in the race. The gas man got a little anxious and went ahead and started fueling the car before they were finished. He spilled gas on the hot rear-end grease and started a fire in the pits."

That ended the day for Allen's original entry, and he was watching the race from the infield when one of Smith's crewmen approached him about filling in for Smith, who, by that time, was seriously overheating inside his car. The decision to bail out of the car was made easier by the fact that Smith had a huge lead.

"I had driven some for Jack before and had done some work for him, so he trusted me," said Allen, now 76.

Allen quickly agreed. Smith dropped into the pits with a three-lap lead—not unusual in those days—on lap 292, and the driver change was made in seconds. Allen returned to the track still in first place and stayed there the rest of the day.

He finished two laps in front of second-place Fireball Roberts and thus became the first driver to take the checkered flag at Bristol. NASCAR rules, however, put the victory in the hands of the driver who started the race in the car, so Smith is listed as the victor.

It was an unusual victory lane, as both Smith and Allen celebrated. More importantly for Allen, who was trying to keep his own racing operation afloat, it was a big payday. Smith won $3,025 and gave Allen a healthy share of the first-place prize.

"They paid off at the track after the race in those days, and Jack said, 'Let's go pick up our money,'" Allen said. "I don't remember how much it was, but I really needed the money at the time. I appreciated the opportunity.

"Sometimes in those days, when a driver needed a relief driver early in the race and they had a good car, they would get back in the car late to finish the race, but Jack elected to leave me in and share the glory. It was a memorable day."

It was Allen's first visit to a Cup victory lane. A year later, he scored a win of his own, finishing first in a race in Winston-Salem, North Carolina. It was his only Cup victory.

Allen, born in Greenville, South Carolina, now lives in Florida. Smith raced out of Spartanburg, South Carolina, and won 21 races in a Cup career that began with NASCAR's first season (1949) and ended in 1964. He died in 2001.

The Bristol track honored Allen many years after that first race by presenting him with a trophy for being the "first driver to take the checkered flag" at BMS.

81 Mark Martin

Of the thousands of drivers who have competed at the top level of stock car racing over the years, few have earned as much respect inside NASCAR garage areas as Mark Martin.

The diminutive native of Batesville, Arkansas, made his first Sprint Cup start in 1981 and is still sailing along as a victory contender three decades later. He is known as one of the smartest, most polished drivers in the sport, has been a mentor for many others, and has a title all drivers covet—that of a racer's racer.

He will almost certainly be elected to the NASCAR Hall of Fame in his first year of eligibility—that is, if he ever quits driving.

Martin chose to trim his schedule to part-time status in 2007 and 2008 but found he wasn't happy not being at the race track every week and jumped back in with both racing shoes with team owner Rick Hendrick in 2009. After three winless seasons, and racing drivers less than half his age, he notched five victories.

Martin made his Sprint Cup debut April 5, 1981, at North Wilkesboro Speedway in North Carolina after winning three American Speed Association championships. He finished 27th that day, but three months later, he scored the first pole of his career in a race at Nashville Speedway in Tennessee.

Mark Martin prepares for the NASCAR Sprint Cup Series Irwin Tools Night Race auto race on Saturday, August 26, 2011, in Bristol, Tennessee. (AP Photo/ Lisa Norman-Hudson)

Driving his own car, Martin ran five races that first year, then he raced a full season in 1982, again driving mostly his family's cars.

It didn't work. After running about half the schedule in 1983, Martin mostly retreated from the sport. He wasn't sure he would be able to return with the kind of equipment he would need to show his talent. There was a chance that he had missed his last chance, and that he would be racing short tracks in the Midwest forever.

But Martin's big opportunity arrived in 1988 when he signed to drive for team owner Jack Roush. They scored three top fives that season, and in 1989, Martin hit victory lane for the first time, winning at North Carolina Speedway in Rockingham.

He was on his way.

His wins totaled in the dozens, and Martin became a challenger everywhere the circuit visited. As the sport grew by leaps and bounds in the early 1990s, he was at the forefront, winning races in every season of the 1990s except 1996 and constantly challenging for the championship.

Martin finished in the top 10 in the Sprint Cup point standings every year from 1989 through 2000. The only significant black mark on his career is that he has finished second in points five times without winning a championship.

Some wrote finish to Martin's career after he went winless in his final season with Roush in 2006. He raced part-time in 2007 and 2008 without winning but then rebounded in his new partnership with Hendrick in 2009, when he again finished second in points.

Age—Martin was born January 9, 1959—didn't seem to factor into his performance. Although he has dealt with serious back problems, Martin, his body hardened by a workout program that he follows religiously, is one of the garage area's best physical specimens. He works out from four to six days a week in his home gym and says he changes his workout regimen frequently "to keep my muscles off guard."

Some thought Martin was a fool chasing his tail for continuing to race after age 50.

"No matter what the car is, Mark can get in it and tell you in three laps what he wants you to do to it and then basically crew-chief the car from the seat," Hendrick said. "Matt Kenseth once told me never to let him get in your car in practice unless you want to see him put up a number better than yours.

"He wants to race, but only if he has a shot to win. He doesn't want to ride around out there for a paycheck. Guys that ride around for a paycheck don't drive a car as hard as he does. Get him even, and let him do the rest."

When Martin won in 2009, he became only the fourth Cup driver to win after age 50, joining Harry Gant, Morgan Shepherd, and Bobby Allison.

Although Martin perfectly fits the mold of the traditional racer, he is a different sort of duck. For example, he and wife, Arlene, live not in or near the NASCAR "capital" of Charlotte, North Carolina, but in Daytona Beach, Florida.

Although Daytona Beach is home to Daytona International Speedway, NASCAR's most famous track, and also is headquarters of the sanctioning body, the Martins moved there in 1994 seeking a bit of privacy. Their home in North Carolina was often visited by fans seeking photographs and autographs.

In Daytona Beach, Martin lives in a "fly-in" development where he can park his private plane just a few yards from his house. It's convenient. It's quiet. It's home.

82 Getting Technical

Although NASCAR is headquartered in Daytona Beach, Florida, where founder Bill France Sr. started the organization in 1947, one of its most important facilities is located in Concord, North Carolina.

The NASCAR Research and Development Center, which opened in January 2003, is the facility where NASCAR employees work on advances in safety and technical areas and where competing teams' cars often undergo rigorous inspections.

The center was opened primarily as a response to NASCAR's extensive examination of its safety rules and procedures following the January 2001 death of star driver Dale Earnhardt Sr. The facility's main goals are to improve safety, enhance competition, and contain costs for teams.

The R&D Center is located on 16 acres near Charlotte Motor Speedway and within easy driving distance of many teams that race in NASCAR's major series. Included in the facility are the offices of NASCAR vice president of competition Robin Pemberton and the directors of the Sprint Cup, Nationwide, and Camping World Truck series. Most of NASCAR's other major offices remain in Daytona Beach, Florida, near Daytona International Speedway.

Included on the tech center site is an area where employees can crash-test cars in relatively low-speed situations.

Although the center has been the focal point for numerous safety advances in recent years, it also has been a "room of doom" for some teams. Typically, when racetrack inspections reveal possible rules violations on race vehicles, the cars are transported to the R&D Center for closer examination. Often, those studies result in fines and penalties.

83 What's In a Name?

Where would sports be without nicknames? Too Tall Jones. Magic. The Babe. Dr. J. Mr. October. The Splendid Splinter.

Stock car racing can hold its own in this competition. The omnipresent nickname in NASCAR always will be the King, the name Richard Petty picked up somewhere in the middle of his fabulous career. It came from that "other" King Richard, of course, but it fit Petty perfectly. With 200 career victories and seven championships, no matter the drivers who come after, he'll always be the King.

Dale Earnhardt Sr. was known as the Intimidator for his fearless, sometimes frightening demeanor on track. The name became so synonymous with one of the sport's most respected drivers that it sold—and continues to sell—an endless river of Intimidator T-shirts.

The name spread to other Earnhardt-related entities. Earnhardt bought interest in a minor-league baseball team in his hometown of Kannapolis, North Carolina, and the team became known as the Kannapolis Intimidators. Years after Earnhardt's death, the Carowinds amusement park near Charlotte, North Carolina, named a new rollercoaster the Intimidator and placed one of Earnhardt's old cars at its base.

Jeff Gordon eventually shed his nickname, and for obvious reasons. In his early years, as he shocked the sport by putting up big numbers for a kid, Gordon picked up the nickname Wonder Boy. He didn't particularly like it, and Ray Evernham, his crew chief at the time, openly opposed its use, saying it made light of Gordon's substantial achievements. Gordon eventually grew out of it.

David Pearson, second all-time to Petty on the Sprint Cup win list, was known as the Silver Fox, both for his prematurely gray hair and for his dependably sly nature on track.

Two drivers who were voted into the NASCAR Hall of Fame together gave each other nicknames. Cale Yarborough called Darrell Waltrip "Jaws" for Waltrip's ability to talk a lot about any number of subjects. Waltrip responded by suggesting that the sport use the "Cale Scale" to rate races in response to Yarborough's comments that some wins meant more than others.

Edward Glenn Roberts was one of NASCAR's first superstar drivers, but no one knew him by that name. He was Fireball Roberts, a nickname he picked up not in racing but as a hard-throwing high school baseball pitcher.

Tony Stewart is often known as "Smoke." Joey Logano was nicknamed "Sliced Bread" because of his predicted superstardom. Ryan Newman became "Flyin' Ryan" and the "Rocketman" for his ability to win poles. Kyle Busch, younger brother of Kurt Busch, naturally became "Shrub," but he also picked up the "Rowdy" nickname because of his adventurous driving style.

And then there is one of the best nicknames ever in NASCAR—Awesome Bill from Dawsonville. Bill Elliott, whose hometown is the small community of Dawsonville in the north Georgia mountains, was given that moniker in the mid-1980s as he stormed through the sport, making the circuit's superspeedways virtually his personal property.

84 A Golden Voice

What are the odds that one of the most recognizable voices on broadcasts of NASCAR events is a guy who grew up on the streets of Brooklyn, New York? His name is Eli Gold, and although he isn't as involved in NASCAR radio work as he once was, he retains ties to the sport he has covered for many years, and his distinctive voice remains one that the vast majority of NASCAR fans recognize instantly.

And Gold's strange North-South axis doesn't stop spinning there. He also is the play-by-play man for radio broadcasts of University of Alabama football and basketball. He is something of a folk hero in Alabama, where his "Touchdown, Alabama!" game call is legendary.

It is no small irony that a Brooklyn kid is not only a voice of NASCAR but also is the radio "face" of one of the most storied college football programs in the South.

How did this happen?

"When I was growing up in New York, I was a big Yankee fan," Gold said. "I lived and died with the Yankees and their broadcasts. You had [baseball broadcasters] Mel Allen, who was from Bessemer, Alabama, and Red Barber from Tallahassee, Florida. So I grew up in Brooklyn listening to two Southern guys. I was captivated.

"Mel went to the University of Alabama and was a former voice of the Crimson Tide. He used to come back and come up to the booth. It was like I had died and gone to heaven. We used to talk about how interesting it was that here he was a Deep South guy making a living and being beloved in New York City, and here was the reverse for me."

Gold, who has homes in Birmingham, Alabama, and Ocean Isle Beach, North Carolina, worked his first NASCAR broadcast in 1976. He added Alabama basketball in 1987 and Alabama football in 1988.

"To say I would ever imagine a kid from Brooklyn doing all this, you couldn't even allow yourself to think like that," Gold said.

Does racing or football provide the biggest charge for the broadcaster?

"The only true answer is that they both do," Gold said. "I have not figured out a way to equate sitting at the 50-yard line for the national championship game versus sitting at the start-finish line for the Daytona 500.

"I'm a racing fan. Before starting broadcasting in 1976, I used to watch racing on *Wide World of Sports*. They both give you a charge, and they're different. When Alabama wins, I'm happy. I live and die with this team. In NASCAR, I don't care who wins. I just want to see a good race.

"I look at it as if they're all important. I owe it to the client. I owe it to the fans. I owe it to myself. I can't afford to screw up. I guess from an emotional tie-in, I'd have to go with Alabama. You see these guys every week. They're kids. You want to see them do well. But at the same time, when I'm broadcasting somebody's first win in NASCAR, I'm as thrilled for him as I am for the Alabama guys winning on Saturday."

On game day at Alabama, Gold arrives on campus early and visits with fans who have assembled near the stadium to tailgate and hang out with friends. He immediately attracts a crowd, signs autographs, and moves on to the stadium, where he has prepared a sheaf of notes for the day's game.

Gold has similar preparations for his work in auto racing. He admits to occasionally approaching the edge of confusing one sport with the other because of bouncing back and forth so often, but there is no record of Gold announcing Matt Kenseth catching an Alabama touchdown pass.

Gold joins longtime NASCAR radio anchor Barney Hall as a distinctive voice calling the sport.

85 A Mountaintop Experience

Phoenix International Raceway in Avondale, Arizona, offers a unique viewing experience for race fans. In addition to the track's grandstand and skybox suite seating, PIR sells tickets on a small mountain—or a large hill, take your pick—outside the track's third and fourth turns. There are no seats, as such; what you're buying for a $35 general admission ticket is a hunk of the desert hillside.

Jeff Gordon operates the tractor for the ceremonial first dig at tearing up the track surface after Gordon won the NASCAR Sprint Cup Series auto race at Phoenix International Raceway on Sunday, February 27, 2011, in Avondale, Arizona. The track underwent a $10 million repaving and reconstruction project. (AP Photo/Jason Babyak)

Fans bring lawn chairs, beanbags, and other sorts of seats, along with small tents, drink coolers, etc., and enjoy the track's races from an unusual viewpoint.

The area's official name is Monument Hill, but it's been known as Rattlesnake Hill for decades by track visitors. There's been a rumor—one that has lasted years—that the track performs a safety-first "rattlesnake sweep" of the hill prior to speedway events, but a track spokesman dismissed that as a myth.

The desert terrain of the hillside perhaps created the rattlesnake idea, one that fans like to talk about but don't necessarily want to experience.

Capacity on the hillside is 6,700. Plus a cactus or three.

86 Yes, There Is a Real Duck

NASCAR drivers become linked to their car numbers. The 43 always will be Richard Petty, the 3 is Dale Earnhardt Sr., and Jeff Gordon is stamped with the 24.

The same concept often is true with sponsors. Earnhardt became synonymous with GM Goodwrench, Petty with STP, and Rusty Wallace with Miller beer.

Carl Edwards has carried AFLAC insurance on his Roush Fenway Racing cars, and that means numerous encounters with that duck. The AFLAC duck—the one that quacks on the company's commercials.

The duck rides along as part of the design scheme on Edwards' cars, and it is pictured in publicity photos and team printed materials.

And, contrary to the perception of many, the duck is real.

So real, in fact, that there is more than one of him.

And the ducks are professionals. During a long photo shoot, they pose for hundreds of shots, the web of photographer lights flashing time after time with no apparent panic or temporary blindness setting in.

A makeup artist, photographer's assistants, sponsor representatives, and assorted hangers-on flit around Edwards, making sure everything is just right during the shoot and occasionally cleaning up duck poop. These are the hazards of having an animal-centric sponsor.

Six long hours later, the session is over, and about 2,000 images of Edwards—some with duck, some duckless—have been recorded for posterity. And for sponsor paraphernalia.

87 The Longest Day

There are long races—and then there is the Coca-Cola 600. It consists of 400 laps around Charlotte Motor Speedway, and it is one of the most punishing days of the NASCAR season. No other Sprint Cup race approaches its distance. It's one of the longest races in the world—in fact, it once was known as the World 600.

Bruton Smith and Curtis Turner, the builders of Charlotte Motor Speedway, tacked that name on their marquee race when the track opened in 1960. Although some 500-mile races at shorter tracks have lasted longer, the 600 quickly became the definition of the endurance run for NASCAR racers. They drive and drive and drive—and still 200 miles remain.

After the track survived early financial troubles, the 1970s saw the track start building toward becoming one of the sport's showplaces, the status of the 600 grew, becoming one of the season's major events. Charlotte was considered a top stop on the tour, along with Daytona, Darlington, and Talladega.

More than a half-century after that first race, the 600—now the Coca-Cola 600—remains one of a handful of standout races that teams—and many fans—mark as red-letter days on their calendars. It is as much a test of survival as skill, and the race-day transition from day to night, a relatively new concept in the 600's history, has changed the name of the game for all involved.

In the beginning, it was a race. Now it's an event. A festival.

After the track installed lights in 1992, it moved the 600's starting time from midday to late afternoon, meaning drivers and crew chiefs must wrestle with the ways the track surface changes from afternoon to evening. A car that is sublime at the start of the race might stink by evening's end.

Although the race has been celebrated as one of NASCAR's most important for many years, it almost never got off the ground. The inaugural 600 was scheduled for May 29, 1960, but it was postponed to June 19 by a wild assortment of problems all linked to track construction difficulties and cost overruns. One of the major construction problems involved the removal of bedrock that the builders had not anticipated during the long construction process.

When the track finally opened, more trouble awaited. The brand new track surface cooked under the June heat, and chunks of the track flew into the air during the race. Some teams put wire screens in front of their cars to protect their radiators from debris, an addition that would be quite illegal—not to mention very ugly—in today's racing.

Jack Smith, a tough short-track driving star from Spartanburg, South Carolina, had the day's best car and probably should have won the race, but a rock ruptured his gas tank after he had led 198 laps. His crew tried to stop the flow from the leak with rags, but that didn't work and he parked his car.

"The track was just coming apart," Smith remembered in an interview many years later. "Big pieces flying left and right. It was like driving through a battlefield. Everybody was putting all kinds of strange stuff on their cars to get through it."

The win went to Joe Lee Johnson, a 30-year-old driver from Chattanooga, Tennessee. It was only Johnson's second win in NASCAR's top series and he would never win again.

There would be other big moments in the 600 over the years. Both Dale Earnhardts—Senior and Junior—made their Sprint Cup debuts in the race. Senior ran in the 1975 race, finishing 22nd, 45 laps behind winner Richard Petty.

Twenty-four years later, Dale Jr. made his first Cup appearance in the 600. Although his father had run virtually unnoticed in the 1975 race, Junior, as the son of one of stock car racing history's most famous drivers, was in the middle of a media madhouse in the 1999 race.

Budweiser, Junior's sponsor, had a "Countdown to E-Day" leading to the big event, and media coverage was overwhelming.

"I remember a ton of pressure and a ton of nerves," said Earnhardt Jr., who started eighth and finished 16th, 10 spots behind his father, who also was in the race. "I can't recall much else about the weekend, about practice, or even any instance of walking down pit road. I remember being in the car before qualifying and being so nervous about it all."

The 600 also was a key event in the career of Jeff Gordon, who came along in 1992 to challenge Dale Earnhardt at the top of the sport. Gordon won for the first time in the 1994 600.

88 You Gotta Be Tough

For much of NASCAR history, pit stops were handled by crewmen who were mechanically inclined but not necessarily athletically superior.

Those days are deep in the past.

The modern NASCAR pit road is populated by workers who would not shy from being matched up with athletes from other sports disciplines. The typical NASCAR pit crew member is a specialist highly trained in an individual task and physically skilled to handle it with speed and precision. Many pit crew members played other sports in high school and/or college, and some joined NASCAR teams after professional careers in football and hockey.

Most successful Sprint Cup teams employ a pit coach to develop and supervise fitness programs that keep their pit teams at high levels of performance. All major teams have gyms and fitness equipment at their shops, and workouts are part of everyday routine. In a sport in which a second or two of delay on pit road can mean 10 positions for the driver on the track, it's imperative that the six people who work "across the wall" be in shape and in tune.

Ray Wright is the man who keeps them that way at Richard Childress Racing. Formerly a baseball star at Louisiana State University, Wright is RCR's pit crew strength/fitness trainer. He's also a tire carrier on one of the over-the-wall teams.

At the RCR shop, Wright rules the gym area. By design, it's a no-frills place quite unlike the real-world fitness centers that include televisions, relaxation areas, and other creature comforts. The idea is that this is all about work and the environment in which the pit crews must perform, Wright said.

"I've got to try to mimic every condition these guys face," Wright said. "It's a little warm in the gym. It's dimly lit. There are no mirrors. TVs are for the lunch crowd. There's not a nice place to sit. I'm doing all I can to make an environment as close as possible to what they have to deal with.

"It's an intimidating place for a man's ego. And I hope that transfers to over-the-wall."

The world of the Sprint Cup pit stop is one of rapid movement, loud noise, and grungy conditions. The idea is to change four tires and add two cans of fuel, while also normally making an adjustment or two, in less than 15 seconds.

Time spent in the gym trims time from pit stops.

"Our workouts are really hard from a strength endurance format," Wright said. "We need strength and endurance when it gets to be really warm out there. And the last pit stop is the money stop. You have to be ready for that, and ready in the firesuits, the heat, and the stress. It all comes down to that.

"It's a meat market. If you're not performing, you're gone, just like it was at LSU."

89 Be All A-Twitter

The phenomenon of social media has arrived with a flourish in NASCAR circles, and fans can experience it at its most personal at a speedway "tweetup."

NASCAR tweetups are held at virtually every Sprint Cup track on race day, typically three-and-a-half hours before the start of the race. Those who gather at a tweetup are members of the Internet social medium Twitter and generally are hard-core NASCAR fans.

Many of them follow other NASCAR fans, drivers, and journalists on Twitter and share information through the relatively new medium.

NASCAR tweetups usually are organized by Jeff Gluck, the motorsports editor for the SB Nation website (sbnation.com). A pioneer of sorts in the NASCAR Twitter world (follow him on Twitter @jeff_gluck), Gluck attends most Sprint Cup races as a reporter for sbnation.com and is the host for track tweetups, which are scheduled at track locations convenient for fans.

The tweetups last for about 30 minutes. Gluck answers questions and meets with fans, and often a celebrity shows up. Drivers Jimmie Johnson and Jeff Gordon have attended, as have NASCAR chairman Brian France and NASCAR Hall of Fame member Bobby Allison.

The first NASCAR tweetup was held at Atlanta Motor Speedway in September 2009. Three people attended. Two years later, the meetings had grown to around 100.

Tweetup times and locations are available to fans by following @jeff_gluck or @nascar on Twitter.

90 Death Rides Along

From the very beginning, it was clear that racing cars in a close environment, fender to fender, bumper to bumper, at high speeds and with almost non-existent safety devices was very dangerous.

NASCAR's early years were pockmarked by spectacular accidents—future champion Lee Petty brought out the first caution in Sprint Cup Series history in the very first race (1949) by flipping his car wildly—and multi-car, flaming crashes. It wasn't at all unusual for drivers to be thrown from their vehicles in accidents. More than a few were run over on the track. Fire was a constant threat.

Additionally, very few tracks took adequate safety measures to protect pit crewmen, officials, and fans. Cars that tumbled off course were potent weapons.

It was remarkable that more drivers (and mechanics, officials, and fans) weren't killed or badly injured.

Advances in safety (particularly in the 1960s and early 2000s) made dramatic changes, but there is a long list of drivers who died at the highest levels of NASCAR competition. Some were barely beginning their careers; others died even as they were contemplating their departures from racing.

The first, according to numerous sources, was Larry Mann, who died in a crash at the ultra-dangerous circular Langhorne Speedway in Pennsylvania on September 14, 1952. Langhorne, a fast one-mile, earned the nickname "The Track that Ate the Heroes." Mann, who was from Yonkers, New York, suffered massive head injuries when his Hudson overturned about two-thirds through the race.

Many other drivers, particularly those who were killed in the pioneering days of the 1950s, died with little public acknowledgement. Among the early NASCAR deaths were Clint McHugh and Thomas "Cotton" Priddy, who died on consecutive days in June 1956 at the super-fast 1.5-mile dirt Memphis-Arkansas Speedway in Lehi, Arkansas.

Many who died were like Ricky Knotts, a young driver from Michigan. Like so many other short-track drivers with stars in their eyes, Knotts traveled to the Daytona International Speedway in February 1980 with big ideas. He planned to qualify for the Daytona 500 and to excite the folks back home with a decent finish in his sport's biggest race.

Knotts had no experience—and certainly no expertise—in big-time superspeedway racing, but he and his family had sewn together enough funding to get a car, make the trip to Florida, and try to qualify for the 500.

Knotts, his father, Richard, and a few of their friends arrived in Daytona Beach and got the car ready. He lined up in one of the two qualifying races for the 500, hoping to finish high enough to make the field for the big race and take home some significant money to move along his young career.

But Knotts, only 28, would not live to see the sunset that day. During the qualifier, he lost control of his car in a multi-car crash and slammed head-on into an inside wall near the track trioval. Officials said he died instantly. Videotapes of the gruesome accident were destroyed.

Richard Knotts and those who had traveled to Daytona with Ricky had no idea what to do next. Suddenly, his son was gone, virtually before anyone in the larger racing community had had time to meet him.

Veteran driver A.J. Foyt volunteered to arrange to have Knotts' body shipped home to Michigan.

A day that started with promise ended in sorrow.

The racing went on. As it would after the deaths of Joe Weatherly and Fireball Roberts, Tiny Lund and Adam Petty, Kenny Irwin Jr. and Dale Earnhardt Sr.

91 Kevin Harvick

A victory in any Sprint Cup race is a moment to be celebrated for the driver, his family, team members, the team owner, and all the hangers-on who claim attachment to the team. Champagne flows, hugs are exchanged, thousands of photographs are shot, and virtually everyone within striking distance is soaked in a shower of assorted beverages.

It's a mess, but it's a fun mess.

But few victories ever will match the pure and deep emotion attached to Kevin Harvick's win in the Cracker Barrel 500 on March 11, 2001, at Atlanta Motor Speedway.

The sport was still consumed in grief because of the death of superstar Dale Earnhardt Sr. the previous month in the Daytona 500. Harvick, then barely a regular in the Nationwide Series, had been named by team owner Richard Childress to replace Earnhardt in the newly numbered 29 Richard Childress Racing Chevrolet.

It was the opportunity of a lifetime for Harvick, but it came with untold pressure. Following Earnhardt in the driver's seat was similar to following Bear Bryant on the football sidelines at Alabama or replacing Joe Montana with the San Francisco 49ers.

The Atlanta race, the fourth of the season after Daytona had opened the year, became a battle between Harvick and Jeff Gordon, and their last-lap confrontation for the win was a classic. They crossed the finish line side by side, with Harvick taking the victory by inches. The official margin of victory was .006 of a second, and it took NASCAR's computers a few seconds to declare Harvick the winner.

In the RCR pit areas, chaos erupted. There was an uninhibited and wildly emotional celebration, Harvick's win lifted—at least for a time—some of the shroud of sadness that had covered the team since Earnhardt's death. Tears flowed freely. Even the team's big and tough gasman, Danny "Chocolate" Myers, one of Earnhardt's closest friends, cried.

Harvick was awash in the emotion of the moment. "I think there was a higher power who wanted to see that outcome," he said.

Childress, who had partnered with Earnhardt to build one of the sport's greatest organizations, winning six championships along the way, said he felt the late driver's presence at the finish.

On October 7, 2011, Kevin Harvick gets ready to practice for the Hollywood Casino 400 race at the Kansas Speedway in Kansas City, Kansas. (Cal Sport Media via AP Images)

"I just looked up in the sky and said, 'I need your help, old buddy,'" Childress said. "And he was there. I could see his mustache break out in that big old smile."

92 Pitting For Film

Modern television viewers have become accustomed to seeing auto racing from every conceivable angle thanks to the ingenuity of technicians who have figured out ways to install tiny but remarkably revealing cameras in numerous places.

Fans can watch drivers from several camera viewpoints inside the car. A camera positioned to the right of the driver shows gearshift changes, the driver wrestling the steering wheel, and the driver's body bobbing in crashes. Another camera focuses on the driver's feet and shows the practiced footwork needed on the brakes and accelerator to move around road courses with efficiency.

Cameras mounted on the roof, front, and rear of the cars show competition from every angle, and networks have even planted small cameras in tracks' asphalt surfaces to show the cars rolling over.

The in-car camera revolution began in earnest in the late 1970s as networks became interested in broadcasting more and more NASCAR races—and more and more of each race. Until that time, race broadcasts consisted mainly of the closing portions of races.

There was a precedent for all this, however, and a driver named Larry Frank was at the middle of it.

In the 1964 and 1965 NASCAR seasons, Frank carried bulky film cameras mounted on the front and rear of his 1964 Ford during races to film action for *Red Line 7000*, a mostly forgettable Paramount Pictures movie about NASCAR.

Paramount's large cameras—much bigger and much less technically precise than the hummingbird-size units in use in the modern era—were mounted on the left front and rear deck of Frank's car.

This didn't create the ideal aerodynamic situation, but as Frank pointed out, the cars competing in those days weren't sleek, slice-through-the-air models, anyway.

"The cars were not as streamlined then," Frank said. "We used the real stock bodies, and we didn't know that much about aerodynamics. We were just learning how to cheat a little bit, tucking the bumpers back up close to the car and getting doors and quarter-panels adjusted so that they made a straight line, making the air flow better.

"So the cameras weren't as big a deal as they would be now."

Frank was the moviemakers' man on the track from July 1964 to May 1965, filming the competition on track at numerous races. The biggest difference between then and now camera-wise is that Frank's cameras carried film, so he had to drop into the pits about every 10 laps to change canisters.

Obviously, that made him something less than a victory threat. But not to worry. Frank was paid well for his labor. He operated his team on a limited budget, and the $12,000 check he received was a big boost.

"I felt like I had sacrificed and gave away a year in which I was capable of winning," Frank said. "But it helped me out a lot. The crew got to eat regular meals and sleep on real beds for a change."

Despite running many laps with the cameras sitting in vulnerable spots, Frank said he drove through the filming period without damaging any cameras.

Not that he didn't get the chance.

In the last practice before the 1964 Southern 500 at Darlington Raceway, one of the circuit's most dangerous tracks, Frank lost his

Can You Hear Me Now?

Radio communications are a given in modern NASCAR racing. During races, drivers can talk to crew chiefs, crew chiefs can communicate with team owners, and spotters high atop grandstands can tell drivers about on-track hazards. And fans, using radio scanners, can listen to all of it.

This now-critical part of racing apparently started in 1952, when two-way radio communication was used for the first time in a NASCAR event.

It occurred on the old Daytona beach-road course along the Atlantic shoreline. Driver Al Stevens used a radio during a Modified-Sportsman race to talk to team owner Cotton Bennett.

Stevens finished third—but started something of a revolution.

brakes in the first turn and slammed into the guard rail. The car's front end was crumpled, but the camera survived.

"I was worried about the camera," Frank said. "I knew we could fix the car."

At the Riverside International Raceway road course, Frank accidentally got some great footage. "Somebody in front of me hit one of the tire barriers at Riverside and sent a tire right through my windshield," he said. "The camera caught the whole thing. You can see the tire coming right at you. They didn't use that in the movie. I never figured out why."

A technician turned one of the cameras sideways with the intent of getting some high-speed shots of the grandstand crowd during a race at Daytona International Speedway. That plan was foiled when the changed mounting of the camera changed the air flow over the car during a practice run and sent Frank into a slide.

"We didn't do that again," he said.

The movie was not well-received, although the action shots Frank delivered were remarkable for that time. James Caan and Laura Devon starred in the movie, which was promoted as a story of "three girls who lose their hearts to race car drivers."

93 Earnhardt's Death Sparks Safety Advances

It was the darkest Sunday in NASCAR history.

On February 18, 2001, stock car racing lost an icon when Dale Earnhardt Sr., working class hero and one of the sport's all-time great drivers, was killed in an accident on the last lap of the Daytona 500.

Newspaper headlines the next day called it Black Sunday. Fans lingering in the grim aftermath of the race in Daytona Beach built bonfires inside and outside the track and gathered to commiserate over their loss. Sports radio call-in shows answered calls from the grieving.

At Dale Earnhardt Inc., Earnhardt's huge racing shop in Mooresville, North Carolina, an impromptu memorial formed as fans left flowers, photos, speedway programs, caps, T-shirts, and letters to their hero.

The next week, *Time* magazine put Earnhardt on its cover.

In a brief moment of violence in the fourth turn of its biggest race, NASCAR had lost one of its major stars. Ironically, Earnhardt's death was the event that fed fire to a movement that vastly improved safety in NASCAR racing.

Earnhardt's death was the last in a series of four fatal accidents that ripped into NASCAR's heart. Adam Petty, grandson of the sport's legendary king, Richard Petty, died in a crash at New Hampshire Motor Speedway in May 2000. Two months later, Kenny Irwin Jr. lost his life in a similar accident at the same facility. In October of the same year, Tony Roper was killed in a Truck Series race at Texas Motor Speedway.

In June 2000, between the deaths of Petty and Irwin, future Cup champion Jimmie Johnson escaped injury in a spectacular crash on the road course at Watkins Glen, New York. Johnson's

Busch (now Nationwide) Series car rolled off course at near full speed, crossed a grassy area without slowing, and slammed head-on into a foam barrier fronting the main fence. It was a frightening moment, and Johnson celebrated his great escape by climbing from the car and raising both arms into the air.

The Petty, Irwin, and Roper deaths churned concern in NASCAR circles. The Petty and Irwin crashes were the topics of most discussion because both occurred at New Hampshire and both drivers lost their lives in accidents that involved sudden impact with the track's concrete walls.

Because of fear about stuck throttles possibly contributing to the deaths of Petty and Irwin, switches to immediately stop engines were added to car steering wheels to give drivers a little more protection. Some drivers began wearing HANS (Head and Neck Support) devices to support their upper bodies in crashes.

But it was the Earnhardt death that launched NASCAR on a dedicated journey to improve safety in the sport. Considered invincible, Earnhardt died in his sport's most famous race, and ironically, became the first driver to be killed in the 500, although dozens of competitors had lost their lives at Daytona over the years.

Earnhardt's death thrust NASCAR into a harsh spotlight. As NASCAR chairman Bill France Jr., Daytona 500 winner Michael Waltrip, and others answered questions at a news conference the day after Earnhardt's death, plans had begun to accelerate NASCAR's safety initiatives. The sanctioning body had come under heavy media criticism for slow movement in that area, and work on bigger technological advances gained steam.

During the months to come, NASCAR underwent a safety revolution, and the results became clear as time passed. Over the course of the next decade, there were no fatal accidents or serious injuries in NASCAR major-series events.

In 2002, the HANS devices, already used by some drivers, became mandatory. They were adamantly opposed by some participants, in particular star driver Tony Stewart, but the devices quickly proved their worth.

SAFER barriers, so-called "soft walls" that absorbed much of the force of car impact during accidents, were introduced at Indianapolis Motor Speedway in 2002 and eventually were added to every NASCAR track. The barriers have greatly reduced the possibility of serious injury in wrecks.

In 2005, NASCAR made full-face helmets mandatory. Over most of NASCAR history, drivers had worn open-face helmets with goggles. The bigger helmets had been available for years before Earnhardt's death, but he rejected them outright.

"He wasn't going to wear a full-face helmet," said Ty Norris, who was the general manager of Earnhardt's team in 2001. "He hated them. He had this theory that the weight of the helmet was too great for your neck to handle in an accident. He wasn't going to wear a HANS device. He hated them."

Earnhardt also didn't like the new cocoon-type driver seats that were being developed at the end of the 1990s. "I don't need a baby seat," he said.

The most public result of Earnhardt's death was NASCAR's decision to develop the so-called Car of Tomorrow, a car with a larger cockpit area, a driver's seat closer to the center of the vehicle, and so-called crush panels of absorbent materials added to the frames. The car debuted in 2007 and was criticized by drivers for its relatively poor racing profile, but modifications since then have made it a more competitive vehicle.

Earnhardt's death was a linchpin in practically every decision NASCAR eventually made about safety.

"You just can't imagine that a guy like Dale Earnhardt was killed," driver Jeff Burton said. "It's hard to even fathom. Of all people, you'd think there was no way you could kill that man. He meant so much to our sport—still does. To lose him was just an unbelievable feeling.

"His death created a scenario where you couldn't ignore it any longer. I wasn't ignoring it. I was hearing when those young guys got killed that they were skinny and their necks weren't strong enough. That's insane. It didn't make any sense to me. When it happened to him, okay, now there is no more excuse."

After all the safety-related changes, the proof is in the results. NASCAR's safety record over the last decade is exemplary.

Some examples:

- April 2009—Carl Edwards flipped his car and flew into the outside catchfence at Talladega Superspeedway as he tried—unsuccessfully—to hold off Brad Keselowski at the race finish. Edwards jumped from the battered car and—to get a laugh—ran across the finish line, unhurt.

- August 2010—Elliott Sadler plowed head-on into an inside wall at Pocono, and the impact ripped the engine from his car. No injuries.

- March 2008—Jeff Gordon made brutal contact with an inside wall—one later bolstered by a SAFER wall addition—at Las Vegas Motor Speedway after spinning. He was shaken but had no serious injuries.

- April 2008—In one of the most spectacular crashes in recent NASCAR history, Michael McDowell rolled and tumbled at Texas Motor Speedway. He walked away.

- August 2009—Kasey Kahne, Sam Hornish Jr., Burton, and Gordon crashed hard in an extended chain-reaction wreck at Watkins Glen. No injuries.

Of course, every race holds the possibility of serious injury or death. But the odds for drivers are much better these days.

"It's sad that we had to lose an icon like Dale Earnhardt for the sport to be so much safer and better for all the drivers," said Richard Childress, Earnhardt's longtime team owner. "If anything good comes out of something as tragic as that, it's that we do have safer race cars and safer race tracks."

94 The Ultimate Red Flag

It's sometimes said that progress doesn't stop for the living or the dead. That doesn't work in all places and in all cases and certainly not in the history of one of NASCAR's classic short tracks—Hickory Motor Speedway in Hickory, North Carolina.

A .363-mile asphalt oval that once was on the Sprint Cup schedule and more recently was part of the Nationwide Series tour, Hickory opened in 1951 and was a training ground for many drivers who became stars in Cup racing.

Hickory produced the bumping and banging and difficult passing scenarios of many other small NASCAR ovals, but it stood out from the crowd for a very unusual reason. The track is located adjacent to a huge cemetery—Catawba Memorial Park, and on the occasions when a funeral at the cemetery coincided with a race at the speedway, track officials would halt the race under a red flag until the memorial service at the cemetery was completed.

This happened at least once during a Sprint Cup (then Grand National) race at the track, said retired driver Ned Jarrett, who was the general manager at the speedway from 1967 to 1976.

"The lower part of the cemetery is within 200 yards of the track [beyond the first and second turns]," Jarrett said. "We worked closely with the churches and funeral homes to accommodate the situation. We shut down the track and the PA (public address system) and invited the fans to go to the concession stands."

For a sport built on constant go-go competition, with no timeouts and no "halftimes," it was quite the unusual circumstance.

Jarrett said the race delays often lasted 40 to 45 minutes. Since the race was under a red flag, teams were not allowed to work on their cars. Drivers climbed out of their cars and visited with crew members or family members, signed autographs, and perhaps had a snack during the delay.

"We always told the drivers about it before the race," Jarrett said. "The funeral homes would work with us as much as possible to not have a conflict, but sometimes it just worked out that they needed to do it at 2:00 or 3:00 on a Sunday afternoon. We understood that.

"It certainly made for a unique situation, but I never heard a complaint from a driver or fans. They understood."

95 Sin City or Race City?

People who were around for the birthing years of NASCAR-style racing might be quite alarmed by this statistic—there are now more Sprint Cup drivers from the city of Las Vegas than there are from the state of South Carolina.

In fact, Las Vegas leads the Palmetto State, which used to be the cradle of successful drivers (see David Pearson, Cotton Owens, and Cale Yarborough, for examples), 2–0.

And for another quirky fact, those two Vegas stars grew up in the same house and have the same parents. They are brothers Kurt and Kyle, both winners and championship contenders in NASCAR for years.

It might seem surprising that Sin City, not exactly a cradle of motorsports, could produce two top-flight stock car racers, but Vegas has had its fingers in the NASCAR pie for many years—and that collaboration is growing. In fact, the Las Vegas flirtation with

NASCAR goes all the way back to 1955 when a Sprint Cup (then Grand National) Series race was held at a one-mile dirt track called Las Vegas Park Speedway.

Las Vegas Park opened as a horse-racing track in 1953, but that enterprise failed miserably. The operators invited NASCAR to town for the 1955 race, which was won by Wisconsin driver Norm Nelson in an event that—oddly for Las Vegas, now one of the brightest places on Earth—was shortened to 111 laps by darkness.

The facility soon was demolished, and the giant Las Vegas Convention Center now sits on the site.

Four decades later, racing returned to Vegas. Las Vegas Motor Speedway (its current name) was built northeast of the downtown strip near Nellis Air Force Base. The 1.5-mile track opened in 1996 and hosted its first Cup race—won by Mark Martin—in 1998.

The track has undergone extensive remodeling in recent years after being purchased by Speedway Motorsports Inc. and now is one of the best in NASCAR. It has a unique infield area called the Neon Garage, which provides fans with viewing areas open to the race teams' work spaces, and on race weekends it hosts numerous entertainment activities.

The Las Vegas Strip became even more "NASCARized" in 2009 when the sanctioning body moved its season-ending Sprint Cup awards banquet, one of the highlights of the NASCAR year, from New York City to Vegas. The city, accustomed to hosting major events, went into overdrive with the sparkle and glitz as NASCAR brought its champions' show to town.

One of the highlights of the first Champion's Week was a parade along the Strip. Champion Jimmie Johnson led the way and ended the event with a huge spinning burnout along Casino Row. He virtually destroyed the engine making the tires sing, but there were no complaints from the thousands who lined the streets and those looking on from overhead pedestrian bridges.

The banquet room at the Wynn Hotel is massive, much larger than the ornate but relatively small Waldorf-Astoria ballroom that had hosted the awards function in years past. The room is so vast, in fact, that NASCAR was able to invite a few hundred fans to attend the banquet for the first time.

For a week in which Las Vegas also hosted Cher, Metallica, and the national rodeo finals, NASCAR got its spot front and center.

It seems like a logical match for a sport that's loud and bombastic.

96 Matt Kenseth

Did Matt Kenseth, one of NASCAR's quiet guys, make enough noise to push the sport into changing the way it determines its champion? Many observers think so.

Kenseth, formerly a Wisconsin short-track champion who has built a strong reputation as a solid thinking-man's racer at the Sprint Cup level, is a near-perfect example of what motorsports people call a "point racer."

That designation identifies a driver who is proficient at finishing races virtually every week (as opposed to crashing out) and finishing them usually in high positions. The point racer isn't opposed to winning, of course, but he's happy to string together a bunch of top-10 finishes and occasionally drop into victory lane.

NASCAR racing has been kind to all point racers over the years. NASCAR's various championship point systems have rewarded the consistently solid racer over the devil-may-care driver who tries to lead every lap and win every race and thus often wads up his car in the wall in the attempt.

Matt Kenseth took two tires on his final pit stop and got past former mentor Mark Martin to win the FedEx 400 at Dover International Speedway in Dover, Delaware, on May 15, 2011. (Cal Sports Media via AP Images)

In 2003, Kenseth put together one of the best point racer seasons in NASCAR history. He won only one race but scored top-10 finishes in 25 of the 36 races and ran away with the championship, locking up the title with one race remaining.

Kenseth thus robbed the closing weeks of the season of the drama that would attend a tight championship race.

His performance was mentioned—not by NASCAR officials but by some journalists and fans—as the primary reason the sanctioning body radically changed its championship process for the 2004 season. NASCAR junked its previous system and went to a "playoff" format, one eventually named the Chase for the Sprint Cup. It put the top drivers in the standings after the season's first 26 races into a revised (and tightened) point standings group for the final 10 Chase races, thus making a dramatic race for the championship much more likely.

It was a revolutionary change in a sport that seldom makes them.

Kenseth thus became the last champion under a format that had been in existence since the mid-1970s. NASCAR, seeking ways to boost interest in the final months of the season (when the National Football League and Major League Baseball grab much of the television audience), went in a new and very surprising direction. The France family, which has run NASCAR since its inception, typically is conservative and resistant to change, particularly major change.

And Kenseth was an unlikely individual to be at the middle of revolution.

Kenseth is popular, but in comparison to bigger stars like Jeff Gordon, Dale Earnhardt Jr., Jimmie Johnson, and Carl Edwards, he is low key. Unlike some of his contemporaries, he is not immediately recognizable on the street.

And Kenseth is fine with that.

"It's cool," he said. "I can blend in. I meet a lot of really great fans everywhere, and I don't feel like I'm being hassled. Katie [his wife] and I have never stopped leaving the track or going out to eat or whatever.

"I love it when we're running good and everything's going good. People are always agog over Dale Jr., but for me it's usually related to performance. If we're not running good, I can pretty much lay low and nobody really notices anything. If we're running well and winning, I'm maybe a little more recognizable and there are more people around. It goes up and down, and sometimes it's nice for it to be down."

Built somewhat in the Mark Martin mold, Kenseth is one of NASCAR's smartest drivers and, in the right company, one of its wittiest. His dry humor escapes many, but those within the close circles of his team (Roush Fenway Racing) and Kenseth's other friends say he's one of the most entertaining people in the garage area.

"He's a shy kind of person," driver Jeff Green said. "He's a great guy, and he has a great sense of humor. It takes a little bit to get to know him and, because of that, he steers clear of confrontations and basically of conversation. He runs good enough that he can get wins and top fives, but he doesn't bark a lot to do that. He's consistent all day long, and I guess he's that way off the track, too.

"He has a dry sense of humor. You never know what he's going to say. It wouldn't surprise me what would come out of his mouth—funny, weird, or important. It always seems to have a spark or a kick to it and gets the point across."

Kenseth doesn't talk a lot about himself. But pesky reporters badger him, and he's generally friendly to a fault. He doesn't like confrontations with other drivers, but he hasn't been afraid to point out the failings of drivers like Jeff Gordon and Tony Stewart when he feels he's been wronged. And for a while, he and teammate Carl Edwards were at odds.

"I don't like to be involved in conflicts," Kenseth said. "I don't like to be in controversy at all. I'd rather just keep to myself and go out and do my job and not have any of that, but if you're going to be competitive and you're going to try as hard as you can every week and try to run up front and do all that, it's pretty hard not to ever get in a conflict with anybody. It's just part of the business."

And the point racing? Part of the business, too.

97 The Streak

Jimmie Johnson has been a dominant figure in Sprint Cup racing for much of the 2000s. He set a level of seasonal performance that isn't likely to be challenged for a while by winning consecutive championships from 2006 to 2010.

There has been the thought that Johnson is invincible, that no one could have the sort of seasons he's had.

But when you talk invincible in Cup racing, you must talk of Richard Petty's 1967 season. Petty defined the word that year, winning his second championship and 27 races. Most remarkable? He won 10 consecutive events.

That victory streak will remain a momentous part of NASCAR lore well past Johnson's current mastery of the sport and well past Petty's lifetime. To talk of a driver winning 10 straight in modern times is to get laughed out of the room.

The blue Plymouth that Petty drove to those victories is one of the prized displays in the NASCAR Hall of Fame.

Petty was well on his way to becoming a superstar when the 1967 season started. He had won the Daytona 500 and the championship in 1964 and the 500 again in 1966. But 1967 cemented his role as a dominant figure in the sport.

Petty's streak of 10 straight began on August 12 and ran through October 1—a late summer/early fall of anguish for those who pretended to catch him. He won at Winston-Salem, North Carolina; Columbia, South Carolina; Savannah, Georgia; Darlington, South Carolina; Hickory, North Carolina; Richmond, Virginia; Beltsville, Maryland; Hillsborough, North Carolina; Martinsville, Virginia; and North Wilkesboro, North Carolina.

A Dominating Flock

One of the most outstanding seasonal performances in NASCAR history occurred in 1955 when Tim Flock won the Cup championship. Flock drove in 39 races that season. He won 18. Flock's true power could be seen in the laps-led category. He was out front at the end of 3,495 laps. Second in that column that season was Buck Baker, who led only 808.

It also is worth noting that Petty's wins that season weren't exactly nail-biters. His closest margin of victory was what is now an almost unheard-of finish—6 seconds. He typically finished laps ahead of the second-place driver.

No one could beat the big bad blue car.

After the 10th straight win, Petty marched into the press box for the winner's interview at North Wilkesboro Speedway. He remembered seeing many of the same media people who had covered much of the victory string. "I said, 'How about me interviewing you guys today? I don't have much to say that I haven't already said,'" Petty said.

The streak ended the next week at Charlotte Motor Speedway, a track that wasn't particularly kind to him over the years. Petty was involved in a wreck and eventually left the race with engine trouble. Buddy Baker, the man who ended the Petty march, scored the first win of his career in that day's race.

During the season, Petty broke his father Lee's all-time career victory record (with his 55th win) and won the Southern 500 for the first (and only) time. Oddly enough, Petty didn't win the Daytona 500, a race he claimed seven times, that year. The victory went to Mario Andretti in one of his rare NASCAR appearances.

During the 1967 season, Petty's popularity exploded so much that "Petty for President" bumper stickers began appearing at NASCAR tracks across the country. He signed autograph after autograph at every track, building one of the biggest fan bases in the sport's history.

And he had defined invincible, at least in the NASCAR context.

98 Smorgasbord of Speed

In the beginning, NASCAR was all about dirt. With the unusual exception of the Daytona beach-road course, a hybrid track that linked the Daytona beach sand and the parallel asphalt Highway A1A, most early NASCAR events were run on dirt surfaces, typically half-mile ovals.

Sixty years later, the sport is long past its Southeastern roots and its short, dusty courses. The 10-month pursuit of the Sprint Cup championship is decided on 23 speedways. Using NASCAR's statistical definitions, three are short tracks (less than a mile in length), 18 are superspeedways (at least a mile in length), and two are road courses.

The majority of the tracks also fall into what is known as the intermediate track category, generally those of 1.5 miles, more or less, in length. The longest track is Talladega Superspeedway in Alabama—2.66 miles. The shortest, at .526 of a mile, is Martinsville Speedway in Virginia.

Although Darlington Raceway, which now measures 1.366 miles (originally it was 1.25 miles), was NASCAR's first superspeedway and first asphalt track, having opened in 1950, Daytona International Speedway's opening in 1959 was really the beginning of what might be called NASCAR's Superspeedway Era.

After Daytona opened with the first running of the Daytona 500, there followed in the next decade Charlotte Motor Speedway,

Atlanta Motor Speedway, Marchbanks Speedway (in Hanford, California, now closed), North Carolina Motor Speedway, Michigan International Speedway, Texas World Speedway, Dover International Speedway, and Talladega Superspeedway.

As the sport was changing from street vehicles that had been modified to purpose-built race cars, the track landscape was changing from dirt and short bullrings to pavement and longer courses.

That didn't mean there wasn't room for short tracks, however. Although NASCAR eventually pulled its Sprint Cup series from a considerable group of short tracks, three of the best—each presenting a different challenge—remain on today's schedule.

Martinsville Speedway, which has been on the Cup schedule since the beginning, is a flat half-mile "paper clip" asphalt surface with concrete in the turns. It demands patience, enduring brakes, and good corner grip. A long day at Martinsville involves 1,000 left turns.

Bristol Motor Speedway is about the same length as Martinsville, but the resemblance ends there—and dramatically so. Bristol is a high-banked cereal bowl of a track that produces alarmingly high speeds for a half-mile. Typical Bristol laps are in the 15-second range, while the much flatter Martinsville track is in the 19-second range.

The other short track is Richmond International Raceway, described by some drivers as the "perfect" track because of its medium length (.75 of a mile), its wide racing surface, and its relatively fast speeds.

The series' two road course events are held at Infineon Raceway in Sonoma, California, and Watkins Glen International in Watkins Glen, New York.

Many fans have looked upon road courses as improper layouts for bulky stock cars, and some of their races over the years were little more than long parades. But racing has improved significantly at the two road courses in recent seasons, and their races now are highly anticipated stops on the schedule.

99 A Million Reasons to Win

At the time, it was an outrageous proposition. In 1985, the R.J. Reynolds Tobacco Co., NASCAR's primary sponsor and benefactor for three decades, introduced the Winston Million to Cup racing.

The idea was simple, the execution difficult. RJR would pay a $1 million bonus to any driver who could win three of the so-called Big Four races—the Daytona 500, the Winston 500 (at Talladega Superspeedway), the Coca-Cola 600 (at Charlotte Motor Speedway), and the Southern 500 (at Darlington Raceway).

A million dollars doesn't go very far in NASCAR racing these days, but then it was a handsome sum. (Richard Petty, for example, needed about a dozen years in racing before he became NASCAR's first career $1 million winner.)

The arrival of the Winston Million program was perfectly timed for driver Bill Elliott who in 1985, would have one of the sport's standout seasons. When the season ended in November, he and his team had scored 11 superspeedway victories, but claiming the $1 million bonus was far from easy.

Elliott won the season-opening Daytona 500 and then won at Talladega in May. He thus had two chances to claim the bonus money—at Charlotte in May and at Darlington in late summer.

Tire and brake trouble hampered the Elliott team at Charlotte, and he finished a sour 18th. The Southern 500, at tough ol'

Darlington on Labor Day weekend in the heat and humidity of southeastern South Carolina, was Elliott's last shot.

There was intense news media and fan interest in the Winston Million program as the tour moved into Darlington, and Elliott was ready. He arranged for additional garage-area security to keep the curious away and did media interviews that week on a regimented basis.

The preparation worked. Dale Earnhardt, Harry Gant, and Cale Yarborough also had strong cars that race day, but Elliott held on over the closing laps and won by a second to collect the big check.

More than ever, he was Million Dollar Bill.

Illustrating the difficulty in winning the $1 million prize, the Winston Million went uncollected over the next decade until Jeff Gordon scored by winning at Daytona, Charlotte, and Darlington in 1997.

100 A Shorts Subject

The 2011 NASCAR season opened with a fairly significant but little-noticed rules change. It didn't involve carburetors or tires or sheet metal. It involved legs.

For the first time, you could see them. Well, sort of.

At the start of the 2011 season, NASCAR abandoned a long-standing tradition, eliminating a rule that had made the wearing of shorts a no-no in speedway garage areas. The change was spelled out in black and white under "track attire." The new directive read, "The following are permitted: shorts, short sleeve or sleeve-less shirts and blouses, and open-toed shoes."

Immediately, the job of garage-area security guard became significantly easier. For decades, one of the guards' main tasks was to remain eagle-eyed in case someone might slip into the inner sanctum wearing Bermudas.

The no-shorts rule was an archaic one that should have been dumped years ago, but NASCAR has been famously stubborn in such matters. Only the need to make the garage potentially a more pleasant place for fans who might have access to it—in times of difficult economics for the racing community—finally produced the change.

Why were shorts considered no-nos for so long? Two main reasons: Officials feared that mechanics and others wearing shorts in the busy garage areas could be burned by fuel, hot engine parts, etc. And there was the thinking that attractive female visitors roaming through garage areas in skimpy attire might disrupt the work day.

There was no rush to take advantage of the change at the start of the season. There were a few takers during the first weeks of the season in February at generally chilly Daytona International Speedway, but the shorts look gained traction in mid-year as the tour visited typically hot spots like Charlotte, Michigan International Speedway, Indianapolis Motor Speedway, and Daytona (again).

A few crew members and a driver or two were seen in shorts, but most regular garage-area residents were reluctant.

Kevin Harvick said neither he nor his team members would be making a fashion change. "Our guys won't be wearing shorts," he said. "And have you ever seen my legs?"

Epilogue

101: Fit To Be Tied

It was a season for the ages and a season finale unlike any other. Tony Stewart underlined once again his status as one of NASCAR's all-time greats.

It was NASCAR's 2011 season—one that opened with relative unknown Trevor Bayne, barely 20 years old, scoring an upset win in the Daytona 500 and ended with Stewart outrunning chief rival Carl Edwards in a tense race for the high ground and the championship.

In the end—at the absolute end, in the darkness at Homestead-Miami Speedway—Stewart, who finished first in the season-ending Ford 400, and Edwards, who was second, were the two drivers tied at the top of the Sprint Cup point standings. In a sport that traces its beginnings to the 1949 season, there had never been a circumstance in which two drivers tied for the national championship.

The title went to Stewart on the first tiebreaker. When drivers tie in point total, the tie is broken based on seasonal victories, and Stewart easily outdistanced Edwards in that category 5–1.

The two drivers entered the final race of a 36-race season separated by only three points, Edwards leading based on a season-long run of consistency despite a lone win posted in March at Las Vegas Motor Speedway. Stewart, who had a mostly mediocre regular season, barely edged himself into the 10-race Chase for the championship. Indeed, he proclaimed as the run toward the title began in Chicago in mid-September that he had no shot at emerging first.

That line of thinking ended quickly. Stewart scored his first win of the season in the Chase opener at Chicagoland Speedway and then backed up that run by winning the following week at

Loudon, New Hampshire. Suddenly, Stewart was very much in the hunt for a third Sprint Cup championship.

Meanwhile, Edwards' Chase run was duplicating his regular season. He wasn't winning, but he was stacking up top-10 finishes and moving along atop the point standings.

Edwards finished second and Stewart third in the next-to-last race at Phoenix, setting up a dramatic final week on the south Florida coast.

Stewart rallied from deep in the pack—twice—when he experienced problems early in the final race. The 40-year-old driver ran like a man on a mission, passing cars with risky moves and zeroing in on the leaders.

In the second half of the race, crew chief Darian Grubb put Stewart on a fuel-saving strategy that set up the closing miles of the event. As the race wound down, Stewart led Edwards (in second place) by about a second. The winner of the race would win the championship.

Edwards made minor gains over the final laps, but Stewart led the final 36 laps and kept his margin over Edwards at around one second.

Stewart won to score his fifth victory in the Chase, sending Edwards home disappointed after one of the most dramatic seasons in NASCAR history.

"That's as hard as I can drive," said Edwards, who was among the first in a long line of people to congratulate Stewart after the race.

The championship is the third for Stewart, who described the final weeks of the season rather appropriately after posing for hundreds of photos with his latest trophy, "If you didn't think this was one of the most exciting Chases to watch from a fan standpoint, you've got to go to a doctor immediately and get checked out."

Bibliography

Edelstein, Robert. *Full Throttle: The Life and Fast Times of NASCAR Legend Curtis Turner*. New York, N.Y.: Overlook Press, 2005.

Fielden, Greg. *Forty Years of Stock Car Racing: The Beginning, 1949-1958*. Surfside Beach, South Carolina: Galfield Press, 1988.

Fielden, Greg. *Forty Years of Stock Car Racing: The Superspeedway Boom, 1959-1964*. Surfside Beach, South Carolina: Galfield Press, 1993.

Fielden, Greg. *Forty Years of Stock Car Racing: Big Bucks and Boycotts, 1965-1971*. Surfside Beach, South Carolina: Galfield Press, 1994.

Fielden, Greg. *Forty Years of Stock Car Racing: The Modern Era, 1972-1989*. Surfside Beach, South Carolina: Galfield Press, 1997.

Hembree, Mike. *NASCAR: The Definitive History of America's Sport*. New York, N.Y.: HarperEntertainment, 2000.

Hunter, Don, and Al Pearce. *The Illustrated History of Stock Car Racing*. Osceola, Wisc.: MBI Publishing Company, 1998.

Latford, Bob. *Built For Speed: The Ultimate Guide to Stock Car Racetracks*. Philadelphia, Pa.: Running Press, 2002.

Poole, David. *Race With Destiny: The Year That Changed NASCAR Forever*. Tampa, Florida: Albion Press, 2002.

Zeller, Bob. *Daytona 500: An Official History*. Phoenix, Ariz.: David Bull Publishing, 2002.